Musings Of A Native Son:

An Autobiography

ISBN: 978-1-4669-4971-3 (sc)
ISBN: 978-1-4669-4970-6 (e)

Trafford rev. 08/09/2012

 www.trafford.com

North America & international
toll-free: 1 888 232 4444 (USA & Canada)
phone: 250 383 6864 ♦ fax: 812 355 4082

Thomas F. Massiah

Musings Of A Native Son:

An Autobiography

The life and times of a

Canadian Scientist.

~ Dedication ~

I dedicate this memoir to my wife Clemmie, whom I thank
for her continued support and encouragement.

I hope that what I have written, will serve to let my
daughter Sharleen, and my grandchildren Adam and Adora,
know something of what motivates the person they call
Dad and Grandpa respectively.

TFM

ACKNOWLEDGEMENT

First of all, I wish to thank my dear wife Clemmie for carefully reading the initial draft of the manuscript, and for providing me with frank feedback on which to base the needed revisions.

I also want to acknowledge the Herculean efforts of my friend Romain Pitt, not only for meticulously reading the entire manuscript and detailing suggested changes, in addition to providing constant support and encouragement, at every stage of the writing of this memoir. Then for personally conveying the manuscript to Carl Thorpe (Executive Director of the Multicultural History Society of Ontario), who also reviewed the manuscript, and made astute suggestions for improving the memoir.

I thank my nephew Alfred Tuitt for his advice regarding the preparation of the manuscript. Thanks also to Raj Daryanani, for designing the cover of this book, and for his ongoing advice during all phases of the project. And lastly, I want to acknowledge the diligence and dedication of Richard Da Costa, who reformatted the entire manuscript (for submission to the publisher), and made valuable suggestions to improve it.

Tom Massiah

CONTENTS

PHOTOS

FOREWORD

By all accounts, Thomas (Tom) F. Massiah is living a remarkable life. I am one of the many who have marveled at his accomplishments. Because it is uplifting and even inspirational, I am one of the few who have asked him to record the basic elements of his life's story. He has finally agreed to write his biography.

Traditionally, it is the author who will approach a respected member of his or her circle of friends and request that they write an introduction or foreword to their particular piece of writing. In this instance, it is I who requested the honour of writing this set piece. This unorthodox occurrence came about because I have known the author for almost 60 years, during which I have gotten to know his story from at least 4-5 different points of view, and also because I can corroborate the authenticity of his many feats.

The purpose of an introduction to an autobiography is, I believe, to give the cultural background and the temporal frame of reference upon which the author records his story- much as an artist would paint on a canvas. So, with that as a guideline, let me get on with it.

Tom Massiah first came down the road of my life when I was five years of age. At that time he was a friend, then a close friend and fiancée, and ultimately the husband and life partner of my sister, Pearl-Clementine. At that time my family lived in rural Quebec while he lived in Montreal which was the metropolitan center and major city of Canada.

Our racial minority status looms large in his story so let me explain. In Chambly, we were 3 black families in a rural population of 4,500 people. Coincidentally, this was approximately in the same proportion (1/275) of the 15,000 black citizens to the one plus million population of Montreal. All of that to say that these black populations were too small to provoke the black-white social friction existent in the United States at that time. In those days, the main ethnic event was between the English and the French speaking populations, while the black-white dynamic was relatively peaceful. The black population clumped in with the English community, however, we tended to speak more French than the white Anglophone community.

Yet, in spite of this picture of tranquility and racial harmony that I have painted, there was definitely a very limited career expectation for the so-called 'coloured' people of that era. Significant in his story is the fact that Tom Massiah was amongst the first to break that black ceiling or barrier by far exceeding the limited intellectual and career expectation for black men of that time. Also significant, I believe, is the fact that he achieved these victories at about the same time, and in the very same city (Montreal) where Jackie Robinson was breaking down barriers in professional sport. For emphasis I repeat, both of these fine black men beat their personal odds at the same time and in the same place.

In the interest of brevity, I must confine myself to several pieces of essential background information which the reader needs in order to better understand what makes Tom Massiah tick.

First and foremost, Tom has a superior intellect. Eliot Jaques, the Canadian political scientist and economist has described 8 hierarchical levels of intellect in humans.

According to his scale, most of us function at the first of three levels. Some highly educated and gifted professionals function at the 4 – 5th levels, while an Einstein or a Churchill functions at the 8th level. It is my strong conviction that Tom functions at a very high level, somewhere just below that of these intellectual giants. I believe that I have seen the face of genius. If not, he is certainly the most intelligent person that I have encountered in my lifetime. As a lifelong student of psychology and medicine, I have tried to look carefully inside the man in order that I may gain a better understanding of the elements of genius. Why? I did this because just as common sense is not common, genius is much more rare.

What drives Tom? It was popular in the 70's to speak of 'a Renaissance Man', the man for all seasons the man who gains knowledge for no other reason than for the sake of that knowledge itself. If that generalization is true, then Tom is the archetypical Renaissance Man. A small example of his many accomplishments is the fact that he has taught three disparate subjects, English, Mathematics and Chemistry (in fact several chemistries) at the University/College level. This, he has done in two different provinces and in at least one subject, in two different languages.

Again, in my lifetime, I have mastered only one broad area, the medicine of surgery. Yet, with his basic science background, Tom can comfortably discuss anything from cardiac physiology to bone morphology, and he asks probing analytical questions, some of which I cannot answer. At the other end of the scale and on a more practical level, Tom is a self-taught musician and plays a good harmonica by ear

Secondly, Tom Massiah has a prodigious memory for all facts and the minute details of those facts. I have been repeatedly amazed by this phenomenon. For example, he remembers every scrap of information, the words to every poem and song he ever learned, and the traffic grids to every city he has ever visited. For the average person like myself, this can be frightening. Can you imagine just how humbling this can be for his close friends when he remembers better than they can, the details – all of the details of their lives, including something they said or did 60 years ago?

I will now offer the reader a small illustrative example of his prodigious memory. Tom encouraged me to go to his Alma Mater, The High School of Montreal. At that time, this was Montreal's largest Anglophone public high school. Our teachers were legendary for their knowledge, their teaching style, their eccentricity and, most of all, their ability to control and discipline young lads who had in common the fact that they were infected with an overdose of testosterone.

Although I attended this school some 12 years after Tom, most of those teachers were still there. Fifty years later for me, and sixty years later for Tom, he still remembers and can mimic all of those wonderful characters, their teachings, their favourite homilies, their habit tics, and even their particular gait patterns. Truly remarkable!

Thirdly, Tom is a brilliant teacher. Not only does he function on a high intellectual plane, he is one of those unusual people who can teach at the mundane level of we mere mortals. It is a generalization that many truly brilliant people are not good teachers because they cannot relate to people of average intellect. A current example would be the Nobelist, John Nash, as memorialized in the recent biography and film-A Beautiful Mind. Because of his ability to extrapolate and communicate the overview, Tom is an extraordinary teacher. He probably honed his teaching skills as a young chemistry laboratory instructor at McGill University. It is very difficult for an instructor to shepherd a neophyte student of chemistry through a lab experiment so that they can 'cook from scratch' and derive the desired end product (a chemical compound) within the 2-3 hour lab period. Generations of premed and dental students (including me) sought out Tom to pull them through.

Lastly, Tom is a great humanitarian. While it is true that the two most important people in his life are his wife Clemmie and his daughter Sharleen, he also cares deeply for mankind in general. Tom is a humanitarian in the sense that he has always given something back, long before it became a popular and faddish thing to do. Tom took me on as a pet rehabilitation project when I was 12-13 years of age. At that time, he was supposed to be courting my sister, however, he found time to tutor me in mathematics every Sunday afternoon. An important part of every lesson involved him building up my self-esteem that I could not only understand, but could also master this subject. It was he who gave me the tools and the comprehension to win scholarships through high school and on into university.

Why does he do these noble deeds? I believe that he gains a personal satisfaction in getting someone to master a body of material, and that he enjoys the challenge of helping us beat the odds – as he himself did. I say this because once Tom takes you on as a pet project; he continues to remain interested in your long-term career development and to make himself available for consultation in your being able to deal with the slings and arrows of every day life. As he did for me, Tom has mentored dozens of people and amongst his most recent challenges, is his young granddaughter, Adora.

By now, it should be obvious to you the reader that this is not simply a forward to Tom's biography. In fact, it is a character study and an appreciation of the life of a true renaissance man. Thank you, Tom. Thank you for your lessons, and most of all, thank you for your life. If it is true that what goes around comes around, then the world owes you a debt of gratitude.

David Allan MacKenzie

A WORD ABOUT THE AUTHOR

by

The Honourable Mr. Justice Romain Pitt

Black people have been so battered and bruised in North America that we understandably tend to recognize only those who are identified by the media, with the *"struggle"*. Thus the media, controlled by the ruling elite, define our *"leadership"*. The point is illustrated succinctly in Randall Robinson's The Reckoning, where he says,

"I have known well by now enough *"leaders"* to know that what passes as leadership is often little more than an expression of egoism. It would appear that a condition of such leadership in the black community is the accomplishment of a relative celebrity that varies directly with rung-level assignment of the leader's status in the broader American community. To Americans, black and white, Jesse Jackson Sr. is a black *"leader"*. James Comer, the brilliant black professor of child psychiatry at the Yale University Child Study Centre, is not a *"leader"*, although he is a seminal and influential American thinker on early childhood education for disadvantaged children. His writings are deeply influencing what Americans know about how children learn."

Having known Dr. Thomas (Tom) F. Massiah from the 1970's, I have always been struck by his remarkable mental acuity, and how he applied his intellect with decisiveness to attain the highest scientific accomplishments, in an environment, and during a period in which even the attainment of a high school diploma was properly regarded as a significant achievement.

There are many biographies and autobiographies about black people in this country, but few about those whose greatest accomplishments are primarily academic or about those who have made significant professional contributions.

Dr. Massiah's autobiography, I believe, will begin to bridge the gap. His is a remarkable story of a Black Canadian who, having lost his father before he was 5 years old, who was not only able to attain a doctorate in Organic Chemistry, (in the two decades following the Second World War), but could also demonstrate intellectual superiority in an atmosphere in which every conceivable obstacle existed

Dr. Massiah, as most great scientists, is economical in the use of language. Since I know that people often use the length of a book as an excuse for not reading it, I want to get the point across that there is no excuse for not reading this book — because it is relatively short. Not only are his experiences gripping, but his insight on important educational and scientific issues, puts this book in a very special category.

I cannot end without noting that Dr. Massiah's wife, Clemmie is what *"Royalty"* should be all about. The young *"sisters"* will find her a wonderful role model.

PREFACE

My story covers 70 years (1931 - 2001), and is centered in Montreal and Toronto — two cities of contrasting ethnicity and culture.

However, before giving the raison d'être for this memoir, I want to comment on the name that I chose for it. That choice was deliberate. I wanted to convey that I am a Canadian born black man, who has reflected carefully about the things that have influenced his life. And I wanted to comment on these experiences accurately, but without rancour, in the hope that my comments will be helpful in ameliorating the status of qualified blacks throughout Canada.

Traditionally, when blacks are recognized as achievers, the recognition is accorded to either athletes or entertainers. But, in 1947 when I obtained a B.Sc. in Chemistry, a Canadian born black (in this field of Science) was a rarity. True, there were blacks in other fields of Science at the time, but usually they were from one of the Caribbean islands. Two who come to mind are Jamaican born Dr. K. Melville (who was the Holmes gold medal winner in Medicine, and a pioneer in McGill University's Pharmacology department), and Dr. E. Melville Duporte, from the island of Nevis, who was Professor of Entomology at McGill's Macdonald College, for nearly 70 years. Dr. Duporte was reportedly the first black to teach at McGill, starting there in 1913.

I knew Dr. Melville, because aside from his professorial duties at McGill, he also did limited practice as a physician, in Montreal's black community. But, I learned about Dr. Duporte only in 1994 (through **Akili: The Journal of African-Canadian Studies**), some 13 years after his death, in 1981. Such is the dearth of information about accomplished blacks, in fields other than athletics or entertainment. Indeed, it is with a view to filling this informational void that I agreed to write my autobiography — because I feel that, as blacks, we can no longer be satisfied with having our history as Canadians ignored. In fact, I feel so strongly about this, that I opted to self-publish this memoir. However, only the most significant events which shaped my life, will be commented on in this preface.

In Montreal (where I spent my formative years and the first 20 of my adult years), my early life was influenced predominantly by the Anglophone minority. They were the ones who erected all of the exclusionary barriers. They were the ones who controlled all of the meaningful jobs. They were the ones who decreed that the only position open to Blacks, was railroad porter (for males) and domestic (for females). Office job? Nursing? Bank Teller? Forget it!

I feel that it is necessary to detail some of the humiliations that blacks were subjected to, when I was a boy in Montreal. For instance, there was a restaurant (Childs) where we were refused entry. And, as I relate in my memoir, my stated goal of becoming a Chemist was questioned (in 1945) by the then registrar of McGill — who implied that it was foolhardy of me to have such a goal.

Yet, despite this unwelcoming environment, some of our parents dared to send us beyond High School, in the almost unrealistic hope that we — their children — might thereby be able to break out of our quasi-servitude. And some of us did. For the first time, we were able to achieve positions (in the Canadian mosaic), previously thought to be impossible.

The late 1940s saw the first Black to be graduated from a School of Nursing in Montreal. In 1947, Maurice Bourne became the first Black to graduate as a dentist from McGill University. Engineers, chemists, social workers and at least one librarian followed. Subsequently, Fred Phillips became the first Black to be admitted to the Quebec Bar in 1962.

One thing that surprised me during this evolutionary period, was the extent to which the Francophone intelligentsia was accommodating Blacks. This was particularly true at l'Université de Montréal, and continued during my time there (1959-1962).

In my memoir, I relate several pivotal instances where I received significant help and encouragement, at this Francophone institution. This help enabled me to complete my doctoral studies debt-free.

Why were they so accommodating? Perhaps they

empathized with Blacks, because they saw themselves as another marginalized group, despite being a majority, in the province of Quebec.

I was part of that pioneering group that made those initial breakthroughs, more than 50 years ago. It was only by chance that I stumbled onto information that enabled me not only to found a self-help educational group, the MNAG (which I describe in the memoir), but also to pursue graduate studies. Information of this type was not usually disclosed to Blacks back then.

The thing that continues to mystify me, is why it is so difficult for some white people to accept the fact that a qualified black person is indeed qualified! I will illustrate my point.

In my memoir, I mention that (sometime in 1958) the Director of Research at Merck & Company, advised me to go on for a Ph.D., stating that this would shield me from on-the-job discrimination. However, this was not the reality. Not only was I treated differently (than similarly qualified, albeit white individuals), throughout my professional life, but I was also summarily excluded from several positions that I applied for, at the Ph.D. level (in both Montreal and Toronto), once it was discovered that I — the applicant — was black! I state these facts, not to complain belatedly, but merely to ensure that the record is both complete and correct.

Today, in Ontario, we see almost unbelievable progress being made by some Blacks. For instance, we saw the Hon. Lincoln Alexander (a Canadian–born Black) become the Lieutenant Governor of Ontario. And there are three Black Senators presently in Ottawa, as well as several Black members of parliament. We have also two Black MPPs sitting in the Ontario legislature, as well as several political functionaries at the municipal level.

There have been a number of appointments of Blacks to judgeships. One which gave me a lot of satisfaction was the appointment of the Hon. Romain Pitt as a judge of The Ontario Superior Court of Justice, in 1994. He is now one of three Black Justices sitting on that court.

Mr. Justice Julius Isaac was appointed Chief Justice of the Federal Court of Canada in 1991. He is currently a supernumerary judge of the Federal Court of Appeal.

A number of blacks have been appointed as Judges

of The Ontario Court of Justice.

But the one problem that has eluded a solution is relations between the Toronto Police and the Black Community. Some 30 years ago, I made several attempts to bridge the gap between these opposing factions, without success. The titles of the talks that I gave are given in the memoir.

There are also a number of Blacks who hold prestigious positions in both the fields of Medicine and of Nursing.

In the field of Education, we now have a number of Black Superintendents, Principals, Vice-Principals and Teachers, something almost unknown when I moved to Toronto in 1966. Recently, there was even a Black Director of Education (Harold Brathwaite) in Peel region.

However, despite these advances, much remains to be done to ensure that more qualified Blacks are included (along with other minorities) for access to the many opportunities available throughout Canada, and especially in its most populace province, Ontario. This will only be achieved when steps are taken to remove all barriers to this inclusiveness.

Removal of these barriers can only be done when there is acceptance of the fact that such barriers exist. This memoir elaborates on some of the barriers that I faced.

I offer this account of my life, as a testimony of how I overcame the many obstacles that were placed in my path — while pursuing my goal (of becoming a scientist), and concurrently trying to make a difference in the lives of those I encountered.

Respectfully,

Thomas (Tom) F. Massiah

IF

If you can keep your head when all about you

Are losing theirs and blaming it on you,

If you can trust yourself when all men doubt you,

But make allowance for their doubting too;

If can wait and not be tired by waiting,

Or being lied about, don't deal in lies,

Or being hated, don't give way to hating,

And yet don't look too good, nor talk too wise;

……………..

Rudyard Kipling (1865 – 1936)

Musings Of A

Native Son

CHAPTER ONE

IN THE BEGINNING

It was around 3:30pm on Thursday, August 06, 1931. I had been playing with several of my playmates, at the corner of Richelieu and Lacasse streets (in Montreal's Saint Henri district), roughly half a block from my home. Suddenly, one of my friends called out to me, telling me that my dad was being taken to the hospital. I ran towards my home, but only got there in time to see the ambulance turn the corner at St. Antoine Street, enroute to the Royal Victoria hospital.

Around 10am the next day, Mother received the news that Dad had succumbed to his illness during the night. Mother was barely in her thirties, and was now a widow, with several small children to take care of. Understandably, she was devastated by the sudden death of her husband, and it was to affect all of us adversely throughout our lives, in many ways. However, in retrospect, Dad's death should not have come as a surprise, in that, at that time, he had been essentially bedridden (while under the doctor's care) for something like eighteen months. Nevertheless, his passing heralded for me (the fourth of six children), the start of a long and at times difficult journey, to a reasonably successful adulthood.

Although I had had a dad for only a little over four years of my life, I believe that a lot of him rubbed off on me. For one thing, Dad was widely respected in the Black-Caribbean community as a scholar, having emigrated from British Guyana (early in the 1900s) to study Medicine. He attended medical school at both Howard and McGill universities, prior to marrying Mother.
Some of his friends even referred to him as 'Doc' Massiah, although regrettably, he never graduated from either medical school. I never found out why. Yet, despite his higher-than-normal education, he spent his all to brief working life as a sleeping-car porter for the Canadian Pacific Railway (CPR). But this perceived failure (on his part) instilled in me at an early age, the commitment, that at

least one of his children would obtain a doctorate, although not necessarily in Medicine. And because I seemed to have been blessed with an insatiable curiosity about how and why things work, together with the facility to learn things, I started my arduous academic journey towards a doctorate, in the post stock-market crash, depression-years of the 1930s. An early picture of Mother and Dad is shown below.

My parents John and Mabel Massiah

CHAPTER TWO

SCHOOL DAYS
-DEAR OLD GOLDEN RULE
DAYS

By the age of three, I could read. So the transition from home to elementary school was uneventful. The school was Lewis Evans — a one-story, rectangular eight – room building, situated at 4275 Richelieu Street, just south of the CPR railway tracks, that walled off Montreal's St. Henri district, from lower Westmount to the north. It was presided over by a dapper, but sadistic principal (Mr. Snodgrass), who also taught grade seven.

From the day I entered Lewis Evans School, until I transferred to Royal Arthur school (at the end of grade six),

I was at the top of the class. Learning came easily to me. I took great pride in receiving gold stars on my report, denoting excellence, and the honour cards given to the leading students at the end of the school year. But my otherwise carefree days at Lewis Evans were affected adversely by my fear of the principal. He seemed to relish instilling fear in the students through his unbridled use of the strap — a practice that I found to be abhorrent, especially since it was being used on pre- pubescent youngsters. Therefore, I rejoiced when this medieval form of torture was finally abolished in all schools.

Ironically, it seemed like poetic justice, that some time after being transferred to another more affluent school, Mr. Snodgrass was convicted of sexual malfeasance, involving some of his students. I do not recall what his punishment was, nor do I remember even being concerned about it.

There is something that occurred in grade 6, which merits mentioning. I think of it, even today, as an act of extraordinary kindness.

A number of black youngsters were chosen each year, by Mr. Dudley Sykes (the Executive Director of The

Negro Community Centre), to attend the Rotary Club's Christmas Dinner, at Montreal's Windsor Hotel. Fortunately, that year, my younger brother Michael and I were chosen to attend. At the dinner, each boy was placed alternately beside a Rotarian. The man who sat between Michael and me, was a Mr. John Mills. He told us that he was the President of the Westmount Rotary Club. During the dinner, he asked us what we would like Santa to bring us for Christmas. I blurted out — a Meccano set — having in mind something in say a 12″ x 12″ box, selling for no more than $5.00 — a princely sum in those days! Of course, by then, I no longer believed in Santa Claus, nor did I have any expectation of actually getting a Meccano set from Mr. Mills, or any one else, for that matter. Still, I went along with what I thought was a ploy on his part — by giving him our names and address. At the end of the dinner, we thanked him for his kindness, and left, never expecting to hear from him.

On Christmas Eve, we were busy setting up our Christmas tree in a wooden box, filled with lumps of coal. Around 8:00pm, the doorbell rang. When we opened the door, a man asked if Michael and George Massiah lived there. It was Mr. Mills! He said that Santa had left a package for us at his home, and had asked him to deliver it to us. Then he brought in a huge flat box that had to be 3ft. long x 2ft wide.

It contained the largest Meccano set that I had ever seen! There were hundreds of parts, a large instruction book, and two wind-up motors. What a gigantic number of objects we could build! A Meccano set like that must have cost at least $100 ——— an unimaginable sum to me, back in 1937. We couldn't believe our good fortune. No one had ever given us a gift that could rival what we had been given by Mr. Mills. As I said earlier, it was an act of extraordinary kindness and generosity.

Michael and I enjoyed our Meccano set for many years. When we felt that we had outgrown it, we donated it to the Salvation Army. We hoped that some other youngster might derive as much pleasure as we had — from Mr. Mills' gift to us.

Now let us return to my public school days, at the end of grade 6. Reluctantly, I had to transfer to Royal Arthur School, in grade 7, as our family had moved into their district.

My teacher there was a Miss Feilde. She had upper-class pretensions, based on the fact that her father was a medical doctor, and that she lived on Sherbrooke Street (near to Guy St.), some distance north of the school. Royal Arthur school was situated below both the CPR and the CNR railway tracks. So Miss Feilde never disguised her dismay at having to teach there.

I adapted readily to the new school, but found that despite my best efforts, I could never achieve a placement of being higher than second in the class. There was a Finnish girl named Sirrkka, who always managed to beat me (albeit barely) mark-wise. But more serious than this was my disappointment in not winning the boy's scholarship, later that year.

In the penultimate report, I obtained an average of 95%, whereas, my nearest rival — a chap named Freddie Grevatt obtained an average of something like 83%. Yet on the day when the final results were revealed, Freddie was given the boy's scholarship (with an average of 88.1%), while my average was 87.5%.

To this day, I wonder if factors other than merit were operative in Miss Feilde's marking. You see, Freddie was white and I am black. Regrettably, it would not be the only time throughout my life that I would ask this question.

As an aside, Sirrkka won the scholarship for girls, and Freddie was awarded the boy's scholarship. So far as I know, neither of them finished High School.

CHAPTER THREE

THE INVISIBLE YEARS

By the time I reached High School (in the Fall of 1939), three of my siblings were also in High School. My older brother James (or Johnny as we called him) was on a 4-year Athlone scholarship at the Montreal Technical School, thanks to the efforts of Mother, who succeeded in obtaining it for him. My two elder sisters (Helen and Margaret) were enrolled in the Commercial course at Strathearn High School.

Except for Johnny, none of us had the wherewithal to attend our respective schools, since fees were mandatory in those days. So my ploy was to attempt to be as inconspicuous as possible in class, hoping that the teacher did not notice me when payment of fees was brought up. My sisters probably adopted similar coping strategies.

Eventually, towards the end of September, we were each awarded a bursary from the school board, and our studies could continue.

I enrolled at The High School of Montreal (popularly called Montreal High). There were only two choices insofar as to a curriculum — Latin or Science. I knew nothing about Latin, except that it was an archaic language, sometimes used in medical prescriptions, and in Law. Since I did not plan to enter either of these professions, I opted to study science. But which science?

In our first year at Montreal High, we were introduced to the study of Biology. Our teacher was a Dr. Lead, a newly minted Ph.D. in biology. Over the four years of High School, I received a first class exposure to biology.

We went on field trips, where we collected and mounted many different species of plants and animals. However, despite the excellence of the exposure that I received, in those days, I could not see how one could make a living as a biologist. Of course, today it would be a different matter, thanks to the current interest in molecular biology. So I looked for other choices in the field of science.

In my second year at Montreal High, I was introduced to something called General Science. Essentially, this was a means of introducing us to the metric system, some elementary concepts in physics and also to mensuration. Chemistry and Physics were introduced in my third year, and was continued in my fourth and final year of High School. With three sciences to choose from, how did I come to choose Chemistry, as the career path that I would follow?

The choice was almost accidental. Each of our laboratory-based science courses required that the student pay something called 'caution money' as insurance against breakage of laboratory equipment. I didn't have 'caution money' (or any other kind of money) for any of the courses. Dr. Guest, the chemistry teacher 'forgave' my chemistry course 'caution money'. I felt indebted to him because of this, and thereafter took a special interest in doing well in the chemistry courses that he taught. Later, at university, I discovered Organic Chemistry, which became my professional life's primary pursuit. But I am getting a little ahead of myself.

There were several teachers at Montreal High, as

well as events there that had a lasting influence on my life.

Aside from Drs. Lead and Guest, Messers. McGarry, Reeves and McBain all were important influences in my development — each in a different way.

Mr. McGarry taught French in grade 10. He was a very competent teacher, having been the recipient of a prize that enabled him to study in France. But this is not what constituted how he influenced me most. It was how he explained Shakespeare's peerless stature as a dramatist, to me. I had asked Mr. McGarry why Shakespeare was held in such high esteem, since I could not find anything appealing in any of his plays (such as A Midsummer Nights' Dream, and The Merchant of Venice for example) that I had read up till then. His explanation went something like this. He said,….

"If I were to ask you to draw a man, you would probably draw me a stick-figure representation, and label it 'Man'. But if I asked Rembrandt to draw a man, he would draw a figure with depth, passion and sensitivity.

Well that is the difference between Shakespeare and other dramatists."

From that time on, I have been able to read and

really enjoy Shakespeare, thanks to the perspective given me by Mr. McGarry.

Mr. Reeves was my homeroom teacher in both grades 10 and 11. It was he who instilled in me the love of mathematics that I have retained to this day.

Then there was Mr. McBain. He was a rather eccentric English teacher, whom the students called 'Cuckoo McBain'. He was also rabidly anti-Semitic, despite his constant disclaimer -----

"Boys…On the staff they say that I'm anti-Semitic. No; no such thing! I just don't like the people!"

Despite his obvious prejudice, he was also an excellent teacher of English, and especially of English composition. Whatever skills I have as a writer, started under his tutelage. Every day, he would announce in class that our assignment was to write a composition, and he would hand out over-size sheets of foolscap paper. Then he would destroy our completed essays by awarding marks such as minus 20, (out of a 100). It was infuriating, but it worked in the long run. He confessed to me using this ploy as a stimulant, during my High School graduation ceremony.

Montreal High was a strictly non co-educational school. The student body numbered 1200 boys, and was comprised of representatives of every nationality in Europe, together with a few Chinese students. There were but six black students in this very diverse student body. This made for no end of problems for us, in that in those days, we were invariably subjected to being called demeaning names such as 'rastus, coon, lightning and snowball'. Our usual response to the verbal assaults, was to respond with our fists.

One of the Black students who attended Montreal High when I did was Oscar Peterson, who was to become the legendary jazz pianist. Although he is one year older than I am, he entered Montreal High (in 1940), one year after me.

This was due to his having been ill for a protracted period. Initially, Oscar was loath to retaliate to the verbal abuse by some of the white students, demurring that he was a pianist, and therefore could not be involved in fisticuffs. However, later that year he changed, and became proficient at using his fists to redress the name–calling and other racial barbs, as did the other black students.

Contemporaneously, Maynard Ferguson (who later achieved fame as a jazz trumpet and French Horn player) and his brother Percy (in whose band Oscar made his professional debut), were attendees at Montreal High. So Jazz was definitely a hallmark of my high school days.

The strap ----that abhorrent relic of my public school days---- achieved vaunted status at Montreal High. It was used so extensively, that the teachers almost had to make a reservation to access it. One teacher announced to his class (on the first day of school) that he planned to strap every student at least twice during the school year. I understand that he did so one and one-half times!

I was strapped unjustifiably (in grade 8) for the one and only time in my life. Then I was informed by one of my classmates (probably erroneously) that my having been strapped, disqualified me from being eligible to write the scholarship exams. So with nothing more to lose, I became decidedly rebellious at school. I vowed that the next time I was strapped, I would deserve it. That never happened.

In fact, what surprised me was that, despite the vicissitudes that I experienced during my High School years (coupled with my at times non-compliant behavior there) I was able to graduate at age 16, coincident with the 100th anniversary of Montreal High.

One factor that helped restore my focus toward school — aside from Mother's unflinching discipline at home — was my entry into our school's Air Cadet Corps. Participation in the corps was mandatory, back in 1942. I enrolled in the NCOs course, and obtained the rank of Sergeant. The following year, I was promoted to Flight-Sergeant, becoming the first black student in Montreal to achieve this rank. Our squadron (#242) was the largest in Montreal, and consisted of 12 flights. Each flight was commanded by a Flight- Sergeant.

A special parade (involving the best marchers in the squadron) was planned as part of our school's 100th anniversary observances. Roughly one-quarter of the entire cadet corps made the cut to participate in the parade. Those chosen were minimally corporals, and each had to excel at marching. Then, which Flight Sergeant would lead the parade, had to be decided. I competed for the honour, and wound up tied with Mickey Stein, another Flight Sergeant. We resolved the impasse by deciding that I would lead the processional phase and Mickey would lead the recessional phase of the parade, which included a rifle-toting armed guard. Thus it was with pride that I shouted out the commands…. "Parade!…Atten Cha!; Move to the right in column of route, Right Ta!; By the left, Quick March!", to start the parade into our school's gymnasium, marching to the beat of the drum and bugle band.

There was a large crowd in attendance. I glanced to see if Mother was in the crowd, but alas she was not there. I had hoped that she would have been able to make it, but something required her presence elsewhere. Nevertheless, even though I appreciated the demands on her time (in her dual role as head of our family), I was disappointed that she did not see me in this my transitory moment of fame. For this was a once in a hundred-year event — the hundredth anniversary of my high school! And I had earned the honour of leading the elite commemorative squadron. So, undaunted, I concealed my disappointment over Mother's absence, and held my head high, as I proudly led the processional of the 100th anniversary Air Cadet parade. Subsequently, I was praised by several of the corps officers, for having done a great job. I was pleased. And I am sure that Mother would also have been pleased.

The following picture is of me in my Air Cadet uniform.

In my Air Cadet uniform

In many respects, my final year of High School, was a kind of a watershed year, for in September of 1942, I embarked on one of the most ill advised ventures of my life. I went west to Alberta, to work as a harvester. Mother did not want me to go, but I pleaded with her that my two closest pals at school were going, and I had promised them that I would go. Reluctantly, Mother relented, and gave me the $10 required (by the Canadian government) as surety for the trip.

In addition, I had to lie about my age, since those permitted to go had to be at least 17 years old. So imagine my disappointment when I turned up at Montreal's CNR Bonaventure station, only to find that neither of my pals was there. I'll resist recounting all the disasters that occurred on the trip, but I will say never again! One of the Harvesters who returned to Montreal on the same train that I did, knelt down and kissed the ground. Another ran towards his father (with tears streaming down his face), and planted a kiss flush on his father's lips.

For my part, the school year was largely a write-off, in that I was never able to catch up with my school work, even though I had been absent for only roughly a month, at the beginning of the term. But somehow I did manage to achieve junior matriculation standing, and graduated with my classmates.

Effectively, in 1943 I underwent a name change. Up to that time, I had been known as George (Massiah). However, I discovered that I had been baptized as Thomas, and that George was not part of any of my given names.

Apparently, it was Dad who began calling me George (pointing out that it was Thomas who doubted Christ), and the name stuck. But I wanted to have my correct name on my graduation certificate, so I made the name change part way through my final year in High School. To this day, my siblings sometimes revert to calling me George (especially during our sometimes-vigorous discussions), even though it has been 60 years since I opted to be called by my correct given name.

In 1944, I took the least expensive way to continue my education, by enrolling in grade 12 at Montreal High.

The curriculum was supposed to be equivalent to 1st year at McGill, and the fee was $100, compared to $400 at McGill. However, I could not afford even that modest fee, and once again assumed my invisible role while still attending classes. I believe that eventually Tantie, (my mother's widowed aunt) paid my fees. I will have more to say about Tantie's involvement in my education later.

Mr. McBain was our homeroom teacher. He was responsible for teaching English Literature and Composition. Our reading list was staggering, involving some 27 novels, as well as a survey literature course covering authors from Chaucer to the Victorian age. We also read some works by French authors (such as Alexandre Dumas and Anatole France), and also the French Canadian author, Louis Hémon. At the time, I deplored our heavy reading load. Later in my life, I was thankful for it, since I feel that it helped in making me a well - rounded individual intellectually.

After completing senior matriculation (in 1944), I entered 2nd year at Sir George Williams College, which was housed in the YMCA building on Drummond Street. I had hope, but I did not have even the modest fee that 'Sir George' charged back then. At the time, Mother was working as a nighttime cleaner in the YMCA. One of her employers there was the uncle of Douglass Clarke, who was then Acting Registrar of 'Sir George'. Mother mentioned to the uncle, that she had a son who was about to enter college. Through his kind intervention, I was granted an entrance scholarship to 'Sir George', which covered all but $70 of the annual fee. Tantie had told me sometime earlier that she would help pay my tuition fee, but only if I enrolled at McGill.

I wanted to go to 'Sir George', because I felt that

that was where less affluent students like me were made to feel welcome. So I enrolled there, with an entrance scholarship, but still some $100 short, in terms of fees and books.

Again I became invisible so to speak. When I finally approached the then Acting Bursar (Henry Worrell) telling him that I did not have the rest of the fees, but that I was expecting to have it soon, Mr. Worrell condescendingly informed me that.... *"It is ok. Your fees have been paid by a white clergyman."* Henry Worrell was a black man. Unknown to me, Tantie had given $70 to her clergyman, to pay the balance of my fees at 'Sir George'. But that was not to be her last intervention in my education. Again without consulting me, she had her clergyman set up an interview for me with the then Registrar of McGill, Thomas Matthews. I attended the interview, even though I had no intention of transferring to McGill. When I arrived at his office, the first question that Mr. Matthews asked me was why had I not enrolled at McGill initially. I told him that I had always intended to attend 'Sir George'. Next, he asked me what I hoped to become.

I replied... *"A research chemist, Sir"*. He looked at me

incredulously and asked…. *"Do you expect to be gainfully employed as a research chemist in Canada?"* I replied with undisguised anger… "Yes Sir, but if not in Canada, then certainly somewhere else in the civilized world. Perhaps even in the Soviet Union!" Of course I was not serious about possibly seeking employment in the Soviet Union. But I wanted to offend him, just as he had offended me. I was 17 years old at the time. That was the first of at least two racist encounters that I would have with functionaries at McGill.

It may have been disquieting to Mr. Matthews (to see from his grave), that not only did I become a research chemist, but that I was gainfully employed as such (in Canada), for more than 30 years. But I am getting a little ahead of myself in telling my story.

In 1945, I had a summer job as a 'chaser', in the tool and jig department of Fairchild Aircraft Limited, which was located in Longueuil, a suburb of Montreal. On August 15, (and without any prior warning), every employee was let go! We were no longer needed. Japan had surrendered, shortly after two of her cities (Hiroshima and Nagasaki) had been devastated by an Atomic Bomb attack. World War II was over!

While I welcomed the end of hostilities, it also meant that I had to find another summer job. It was still six weeks before the resumption of my studies at 'Sir George', and I needed every cent that I could earn during the summer break from school. So I sought the only job I felt that I could obtain, and became a trainee sleeping-car porter with the Canadian National Railway (CNR).

After a brief training period, I was sent out on my first trip (of only two) that I made as a sleeping-car porter. It consisted of a full complement of 28 passengers, bound for Winnipeg, Manitoba. As a porter, you were entitled to only 3 hours sleep a night, and you had to coordinate your sleep period with the porter in the adjacent car. The rest of the night, you were expected to shine the passenger's shoes, clean up the smoker, and do a number of other menial tasks. That after having made a minimum of 28 beds!

And to add to this, invariably passengers would call you 'George' (rather than addressing you as 'Porter'), no matter what your name was.

The only other trip that I made as a porter was to Halifax, Nova Scotia. What I remember most vividly about that trip, was a restaurant (named Norman's, I believe), where porters had to enter through the back door, in order to be served. That memory left me with an aversion for Halifax — a place I would not visit again for more than 45 years.

My brief experience as a sleeping-car porter made me appreciate the fortitude demonstrated by so many black men — including my dad — who had to spend their entire working life as a porter, in order to provide for their family. This awareness of some of the sacrifices that Dad had had to make on our behalf, reinforced my commitment to return to, and do well at school. So, happily it was back to school, at the end of September 1945.

My three years at 'Sir George' were enjoyable. For the most part the teachers were great, although very few of them had PhDs, and in many instances, the faculty was comprised of recent graduates. But the universal characteristic they exhibited was dedication to teaching their students. And I look back appreciatively to the three Pandemic courses (Natural Science, Social Science and The Humanities) that each student was required to take, irrespective of his or her faculty enrolment. These courses were truly basic to a good education. On May 30, 1947, I was graduated from 'Sir George' with a B.Sc. (chemistry major) at age 20.

The year after I obtained my B.Sc., I wrote a cheque for $170 which I intended to give to Tantie, as repayment of the fees she had advanced to me during my student days. But Mother told me reasons why I should not give it to her. So I never did.

I planned tentatively that I would continue graduate studies at Columbia University in New York City. So immediately after graduation, I did not undertake to find a job. Instead, I busied myself with painting, plastering and carrying out other refurbishment of our family's dwelling. One day, during a lull in this activity, I went to 'Sir George' to check on some information that I needed. Once there, I saw that a job was advertised for someone with a B.Sc. (in chemistry) to head up a Quality-Assurance (Q-A) lab. I felt that I had absolutely no chance of obtaining the job, since the only laboratory experience I had was in the laboratories at 'Sir George'. Besides, I wasn't even looking for a job. I was going to graduate school at Columbia! Nevertheless, perhaps simply out of curiosity, I applied for the position.

To my complete surprise, I was invited to an interview with the Plant manager, Mr. Fred Grant, a chemical engineer, who had graduated from MIT. The interview went surprisingly well. We explored a variety of topics, including several non-technical issues, such as my attitude towards the nazi-leaning German-American Bund.

Apparently I made a favourable impression, for from time to time, I heard Mr. Grant say … "When you come in…", but I never let on that I had heard this expression of me being acceptable (in his eyes) for the position.

At an opportune time however, I asked Mr. Grant what was the company's policy about hiring a 'coloured' person. We did not refer to ourselves as 'black' in those days. He replied that he did not know, but would ask.

The firm was the Dewey & Almy Chemical company, headquartered in Cambridge, Massachusetts. I was applying for a position at the Canadian plant, located in Ville LaSalle, a suburb of Montreal. About three days later, Mr. Grant called, asking when I could come in to start work. I had been hired. So, graduate school would have to be deferred for a little over six years.

There had been other Quality-Assurance 'Chemists'

at Dewey & Almy, but I was the first to set up and run the lab on a truly scientific basis. I discarded the trial and error methods of my predecessors. Instead, I derived reliable, mathematically - based methods for adjusting the 130 or so batches of product that we produced each month. During the slightly more than six years of my tenure, our lab tied repeatedly with the one in Chicago, as being the best among the 32 labs in the Dewey & Almy circuit. But this recognition did not satisfy my quest for 'other mountains to climb'. So at one point, I asked Mr. Pearson (the Vice-President and General Manager) for an indication of my future prospects with the company. He replied… "Tom, you have a job for life with us. But you will not be able to do research, because you do not have a post-graduate degree."

Now, I enjoyed my work as a Q-A chemist, but it was not what I wanted to do for the rest of my life. Clearly, I had to return to school for post-graduate studies. But how? That story follows.

CHAPTER FOUR

TO THE GARDEN
~ALONE!

Up to this point in my life, I felt that metaphorically, I had been in a garden — planting seeds that would germinate — producing several career-influencing events in my life. Among these epochal events was my becoming a university lecturer, marriage, my return to graduate school, the birth of my daughter and the obtaining of my first post-graduate degree. But concurrent with this otherwise buoyant period, I was also to experience a profound feeling of being alone — alienated from each of my siblings, over the issue of my marriage in 1951.

During 1948 and 1949, I continued taking additional chemistry courses, as an evening-division student at 'Sir

George', even though I had a B.Sc., and was working full-time as a Q-A chemist. Secretly, I kept hoping that a graduate school would open soon at my alma mater. As I was leaving one of my lectures, I ran into Dr. Madras, one of my former chemistry professors. He greeted me saying, " Oh Tom, I was just thinking of you. How would you like to teach a course in Textile Chemistry?" When I told him that I didn't know very much about Textile Chemistry, he countered by pointing out that I did know a fair bit of chemistry; and all that I would have to do is to apply that knowledge to textile conversion. This didn't seem to be too daunting a task, so I undertook the challenge, becoming an evening-division lecturer (in 1949), at the age of 22. My part-time teaching at 'Sir George' spanned 15 years, during which time I acquired two additional academic degrees.

In 1949, I began dating Clementine Tuitt. She became my wife in 1951. We had met initially at the home of a mutual family friend, when she was 8 years of age and I was 10. She was a head taller than me at the time, and pleaded with her Mom … "…to make him leave me alone!"   I had chased her incessantly during our first meeting.

We met only sporadically thereafter, because she lived in Chambly, a rural town some 20 miles south of Montreal. Our pivotal meeting took place (in 1949) at The Montreal Repertory Theatre. The Negro Theatre Guild was presenting Eugene O'Neill's "The Emperor Jones" there. I had a small acting part in the play, and was also the Guild's business manager. Clemmie had volunteered to help out as an usherette.

[As an aside, The Guild went on to compete in and win the Western Quebec regional drama festival. Subsequently (as part of my function as business manager), I arranged the transportation and billeting of the 40 member cast that traveled to Toronto, to compete in the 1949 Dominion Drama Festival. While we did not win (in Toronto), our leading actor, Percy Rodrigues won the best actor award. He was awarded the Lorne Greene scholarship, and went on to a successful career as an actor, in Hollywood.]

Soon thereafter, it became evident that Clemmie and I were 'an item', so to speak. This should not have been surprising however, given how long we had known and been attracted to each other. In addition, our families were friends.

At first, Mother seemed to agree fully with my choice of Clemmie as my girlfriend. In fact, years earlier, she had often teased Clemmie, telling her that one day, she would be her daughter-in-law. But (in 1950), when I told Mother that I planned to marry Clemmie, and asked for her blessing, Mother unleashed a torrent of verbal abuse on me, that persisted incessantly for the entire 50 weeks that I was engaged. No matter what time of day I showed up at home, Mother would begin her vituperative remarks towards me, about my impending marriage. Throughout that time, not one of my siblings made any attempt to intercede with Mother on my behalf. I felt completely alone — vilified for reasons that I still do not understand.

Was it the fact that I was the only member of my family who had gone to and graduated from college, at that time? If so, then it was a bogus reason for vilifying me.

Had they chosen to, any of my siblings could have gone to college under precisely the same conditions that I had.

No special provisions were ever made for me to

attend college. And in 1951, up to the day I married, I was still living at home (and contributing fully to its upkeep), four years after graduating from college! Or, was it simply that I (the fourth of her children) was marrying first — ahead of two older sisters, and an even older brother?

In a continuing effort to find out the reasons underlying Mother's fierce resistance, I took her out to dinner (more than once during that period) to see if we could reach either an accommodation, or at least an understanding of the root cause(s). But it was to no avail. Mother was unyielding. So I abandoned any further attempts to assuage her.

Mother's opposition to our forthcoming marriage was as hurtful to Clemmie, as it was frustrating to me. What had she done to incur Mother's wrath? There wasn't a scintilla of scandal about Clemmie anywhere in either Montreal's black or the white community. At one point, her parents suggested to her that perhaps she should abandon plans to marry me, as she did not need the opposition that it had generated. But happily, she did not, and our marriage went forth as scheduled. I will have more to say about this later.

As part of my coping strategy (in addition to attempting to maintain my sanity), I began to write a textbook on Textile Chemistry. As I mentioned earlier, in 1949, I undertook to teach a course on this subject at 'Sir George'.

The 50 weeks of my engagement were spent with me preparing the handwritten manuscript, which Clemmie would type on a rented typewriter. How utterly unromantic! And in the midst of my endless torrent of abuse from Mother at home, it was a wonder that I was able to compose anything resembling a textbook. But together, Clemmie and I finished the book. I sent it to England, where it was accepted provisionally, with a request for minor revisions. However, since the prime objective (i.e. retaining of my sanity) had been achieved, I did not bother with the revisions. Instead, I had the typed manuscript bound, and used it to teach the course for the several years that it was offered at 'Sir George'.

Because of Mother's unrelenting opposition to our marriage, Clemmie and I decided that we would get engaged quietly. I tried to come up with a unique place and time to 'pop the question'. The place I chose was the corner of Craig and Bleury streets. The time was 11pm, on July 31, 1950, the eve of her 22nd birthday.

I asked Clemmie … "Veux tu une bague fiançailles pour ton anniversaire?" (Do you want an engagement ring for your birthday?). Without any hesitation, she replied … "Oui!" (Yes!). I hadn't realized that she understood that much French. But she did. So, I gave her the engagement ring, then took her to the Roseland Ballroom (on Ontario Street), where we celebrated our engagement while drinking several daiquiris.

Clemmie and I were married on July 14, 1951. It was one of the largest weddings ever held in Montreal's black community. There were 550 guests. Our wedding party was 20 in number, with an additional 6 men who functioned solely as ushers at the church. The only person who was not in attendance was Mother! And, except for my elder brother Johnny (who was the photographer), none of my family took part in our wedding. My sisters attended, but were otherwise totally uninvolved in my wedding.

I had asked my younger brother Michael to be my best man, but he declined. So, I asked Fred Phillips (who had been my closest friend since I was 11 years old), and he accepted.

Parenthetically, in 1962, Fred became the first black person to be admitted to the Quebec Bar. He practiced Law for more than 30 years, in Montreal, before retiring several years ago.

It surprised me that, despite the fact that our wedding was being held in Chambly — a surburban village some 20 miles from Montreal — all the invitees managed to get there — in all their finery, and on time. This was all the more amazing, in that, in those days, very few of Montreal's blacks owned a car.

Even after all these years, it is difficult to articulate just how alone I felt on my wedding day. But one person was there for me — that person was Aunt Dot — someone that I'll say more about in the final chapter of this memoir.

As Clemmie and I walked back from the altar (after being married), Aunt Dot exclaimed… "Atta boy!". I turned to where she was seated, and smiled my approval of her remark.

Despite feeling utterly abandoned by my family (on this extremely important day of my life), I called Mother just before leaving on our honeymoon, and both Clemmie and I spoke respectfully to her.

My Wedding to Clemmie: (1951)

Next comes the matter of how I effected my return to school. Ever since my conversation with Mr. Pearson (in which he disclosed my limited prospects at Dewey & Almy), the need to pursue graduate studies was uppermost in my thoughts. But how could I do so, now that I had additional responsibilities, as a newly married man?

One Saturday, early in September 1952, I was at a Faculty luncheon at 'Sir George' I told a colleague (Claire Yates) about my wanting to go to graduate school, but of being unable to do so, because I was now a married man. Claire countered by saying…. " I am married, I have a 6 year old son, and I'm attending graduate school at McGill". Astounded, I asked him how he was able to do so. Claire then told me about the fellowships, studentships and demonstatorships that were available to assist in funding graduate studies. For the rest of the luncheon, my only thoughts were focussed on how quickly I could return home, to broach the subject with Clemmie. When I did ask her about it, she said without any hesitation…. "Of course you may return to school. I'll work." She did not even need details as to the financial help available to graduate students, which I disclosed to her later.

Immediately thereafter, I applied to McGill for admission to graduate school, but was told that I would have to wait until the beginning of the next school year, in 1953.

I was surprised that even though I had been graduated from college for nearly 6 years, I was woefully ignorant about the ways available to fund graduate school. I guessed that this was probably true of the other black college and university graduates at the time. The brief survey that I made, confirmed my surmise. So I recruited some 20 or so black college (and nursing-school) graduates, to form an organization called The Montreal Negro Alumni Group (MNAG). An announcement of the formation of the MNAG, with the picture of me (that accompanied the announcement), is shown below.

[The following article was printed in the March 23,1953 issue of The Montreal Gazette]

Negro Youth Group Formed

A new organization to stimulate the trend of higher education among the Negro youth of Montreal, called the Montreal Negro Alumni Group has been formed, Thomas Massiah president of the group announced yesterday.

The aim of the organization is to provide assistance to deserving Negro students.

Mr. Massiah said the group was composed of Negro university graduates who recognized the need for guidance, encouragement and financial aid, and was trying to acquaint students of high school age with the requirements of universities, and the scope of whatever field they planned to enter.

The group would provide a vocational guidance committee, a student coaching body and a committee to provide students with tuition fees.

The president said that the basic requirements for membership in the group were a willingness on the part of the interested person to contribute the value of their education and experience, and to assist financially to the extent of their capabilities.

In addition to Mr. Massiah, the executive of the group includes Roy Rogers, vice-president; Marjorie Mahomed, secretary; Doris Wheatle, assistant secretary; and Owen Rowe, treasurer.

The Montreal Negro Alumni Group is affiliated with the Negro Community Centre, and meets the first Sunday of each month, at the Centre, 3007 Delisle St.

While the announcement provides the bare essentials about the MNAG, I feel that some amplification is needed.

The purpose of the MNAG was to facilitate access to post-secondary education among black high school students, by providing scholarships, bursaries, career information and tutorial aid.

Each member committed to offering tutorial assistance in his or her field of expertise. Tutorials were conducted on a one-to-one basis, and were usually done in the home (or office) of the tutor.

One student that I tutored is Joe Sealy Jr. — currently a well-known jazz pianist and composer, operating out of Toronto. Joe has received numerous awards for his musical compositions. Perhaps the most notable is the Juno Award that he received for his composition, Africville Suite.

I feel that some comment about the name that we chose for our organization is also warranted.

In those days, we never referred to ourselves as blacks. The word 'black' was pejorative to us. Instead, we used 'Negro' — a word which we found more acceptable.

The other matter that we agonized over for some time, was — exactly how should we describe our fledgling organization? 'Club' was considered too trivial, while words like association, fraternity and especially society, were rejected out of hand, because each conveyed an undesired sense of elitism. Eventually, we settled on the word 'group', because it suggested inclusiveness.

I am sure that if the MNAG was being formed today, 'black' would be part of its name. You may ask, why has the word 'black' become so acceptable to my people today, after being considered demeaning and derogatory by us in the 1950s?

I do not know what led to its widespread acceptance by other blacks. But I do know what happened in my case. My acceptance of 'black', as a descriptive of my ethnicity, came in 1971, as a result of a visit to Texas Southern University — a black university, in Houston. While there, I had several discussions with students, about civil rights, and its implications for our people. I learned from the students, that when they used the word 'black', they were referring to a liberated state of mind — and not to a colour! This enlightened revelation caused me to also embrace 'black' as a descriptive of my state of mind — which was now in harmony with that of a significant number of black people. People who had discarded the mental yoke of servitude! People who felt confident that ultimately we will prevail — even in a society where the 'playing field' for blacks is seldom level. Once I made the mental transition, there was no turning back! I was 'black' forever — and confident about our future! Still, it puzzles why — in white America, blacks are constantly relegated to the bottom of the socio-economic ladder. This, despite the recent genetic inference of the sameness of all people[1] irrespective of ethnicity, coupled with irrefutable evidence that Man (as a species) originated in Africa!

---

1 National Geographic, p.42-49; 54-59; 64-75 (October 1999)

Now to continue the story about the MNAG.

Shortly after its formation, the MNAG held a general information (or GEN) night, at which each member presented information about his or her field. Topics covered were educational requirements, costs, assistance programs and career opportunities. The fields discussed were Accountancy, Chemistry, Dentistry, Engineering, Journalism, Law, Medicine, Nursing and Social Work. Fortunately, our information was current, as we had representatives of each of these fields among our membership. The audience for our GEN night, consisted mostly of students interested in these areas of study, and their parents. Overall, I felt that the GEN night was a success.

Funds for the scholarships and bursaries, awarded by the MNAG, were obtained from the annual Scholarship Dinner and Dance. A picture of some of the MNAG members, at the first Dinner-Dance, is shown below.

In addition to being its founder, I also served as the first president of the MNAG. However, some 3-years after founding the MNAG, I resigned over philosophical differences as to where and how the group should function.

MNAG First Scholarship Dinner-Dance: (1953)

To its enduring credit, the MNAG distributed more than $30,000 in scholarships, as well as numerous bursaries, information about careers, and also tutorial assistance, during its 15-year existence.

Before relating my experiences as a married student returning to school after an absence of slightly more than 6 years, I want to digress, in order to tell you about a particularly poignant experience that Clemmie and I underwent, shortly after the beginning of our marriage.

We had rented a semi-basement of a duplex, from a

Jewish couple, Nathan and Mollie Schwartz. It was located in the upper middle-class enclave of Hampstead, (just to the west of Snowdon junction in Montreal). Jews had been rigorously excluded from owning homes in Hampstead. But suddenly, they were buying homes there, principally on MacDonald Avenue. That was where the Schwartzes lived.

Nearly all of the new homeowners had rented out their semi-basements, as a means of helping them pay off their mortgage. However, Clemmie and I were the only black couple among the young basement-apartment dwellers.

At first the Hampstead city officials did not react to our presence, since they probably assumed that we were Nathan and Mollie's domestic help.

But when they noticed that Clemmie and I went out to work daily, they sprang into action. The Hampstead City-Manager concocted a ridiculously transparent plan to evict us. He sent the Schwartzes a letter saying that the area in which they lived was zoned for bungalows and duplexes. Then he pursued his blatantly flawed logic, by stating that since there was someone residing in the semi-basement, the dwelling was ipso facto, a triplex — a structure prohibited by the zoning by-law.

Nathan and Mollie wanted to fight this nonsensical by-law, but we asked them not to do so. Instead, we agreed to move, but it was not because we were afraid of a fight. Rather, it was because Clemmie had experienced considerable discomfort and was catching colds, due to the dampness of the semi-basement. Our moving (under the pretext of acceding to the actions of the Hampstead city officials) gave us a way to avoid offending Nathan and Mollie — a couple we had come to like very much.

The day we moved out, a white couple moved in. There was not a single reaction to their presence, by the Hampstead officials. Nor were any of the homeowners (who had also rented out their semi-basements — albeit to white couples) ever contacted. This episode told me reams about the place of Canadian blacks (including even those who were demonstrably progressive) in the Canadian mosaic, at that time.

Now about my return to school.

In September 1953, I enrolled in what was called a 'qualifying year' at McGill.

This was because I had been graduated from 'Sir

George' (with a major in chemistry), whereas McGill required honours chemistry standing for entry into its graduate school. I was given a very heavy load of chemistry courses, as well as two demanding mathematics courses. Concurrently, I was lecturing part time at 'Sir George', and demonstrating laboratory courses both at McGill and 'Sir George'. All told, I was involved with school for roughly 37 hours a week.

After my hectic 'qualifying year', I was accepted as a graduate student (at McGill) to study Organic Chemistry, under Professor Alfred Taurins. The research problem that I chose to work on under his guidance involved the synthesis of compounds that might be useful as local anesthetics. I made this choice because I wanted to work in the pharmaceutical field after graduation.

For more than a year, I worked diligently on my assigned problem, but had virtually no success. Many times I worked at night, and also on Saturdays. It was during one of my Saturday afternoon sessions in the lab, that a career-altering event took place.

We had been told (by the department chairman, Dr. Winkler), that graduate students could play a radio in the lab after 1:00 pm on Saturdays. So I had taken up a collection from my fellow lab-mates, and bought an inexpensive radio. There were three graduate students in the lab that Saturday afternoon. The Metropolitan Opera was on, and one of the graduate students (from Switzerland), was trying to explain the intricacies of opera to me, while we toiled away on our respective projects. Suddenly, the lab door opened, and a professor (Dr. Hatcher) bellowed at us …. "Turn off that radio!". The Swiss student told Dr. Hatcher that Dr. Winkler had given us permission to play the radio (after 1:00pm) on Saturdays. "I don't care who gave you permission — turn off that radio!" was his reply. At this point I asked Professor Hatcher if he would be present in the department every Saturday afternoon. I did so quietly and politely. Why I asked this question is somewhat irrelevant. But it was simply to determine if we had to get rid of the radio altogether. He retorted angrily that …. "I'm here whenever I feel like it!", whereupon I made no further comment, and simply turned off the radio.

Monday morning, I was once again in the lab with the same lab-mates. The lab door opened. It was Dr.

Winkler. He directed his remarks to me. "Professor Hatcher said that a 'coloured' student was very rude to him on Saturday. Was it you? As it happened, at the time I was the only 'coloured' student among the 127 graduate students in the department. I told Dr. Winkler that I had been present in the lab on Saturday, but denied being rude to Professor Hatcher. I even suggested to him that he question us separately, to determine the validity of our account. He rejected this, and insisted that I go to Dr. Hatcher and apologize. I indicated that since I had not been rude, any apology offered would be a hollow one. Dr, Winkler's final words to me were …. "You will go to Dr, Hatcher and apologize! Your degree could well hang on it!" I was dumbfounded. Here I had given up a good paying job, to return to school, and I was now embroiled in a controversy not of my own making.

After considering my options overnight, I decided (out of consideration for Clemmie) that I would apologize to Dr. Hatcher.

When I went to his office, he was lying on a cot. I knocked. " Who's there?".. he bellowed. I told him my name, and said that I had come to apologize about the

incident on Saturday afternoon. His response was....
"Who're you! I don't recognize you! And I don't accept
apologies from people I don't recognize! You should read
the book "A Man Without a Country! Now get out of my
office!"

I left his office hastily, and rushed directly to Dr.
Winkler's office. I intended to tell Dr. Winkler that he
could use my degree as a suppository! Providentially, Dr.
Winkler had left town and would not be back for 3 days.
That gave me time to cool down, so I never told him of my
suggestion regarding the degree. But the die had been cast,
insofar as McGill and me was concerned.

After this incident, I re-doubled my efforts to obtain
enough results on my research project to enable me to
write my M.Sc. dissertation. Success came when a resorted
to what I have used in problem-solving ever since. It was to
define the problem! As soon as I did so, the answer became
deceptively obvious. And what I had been unable to
achieve in the preceding 18 months, I was able to do in
roughly 3 months. Based on these results, I wrote and
submitted my M.Sc. dissertation. I was granted the degree
'cum laude'. Then I left McGill, intent on pursuing my

Ph.D. studies elsewhere, at a later date, as I had become the father of a baby girl (in September of 1955), nearly 1 year prior to receiving my M.Sc.

Before going on to tell how and where I continued my Ph.D. studies, I want to relate how involved my final M.Sc. year was.

As I mentioned earlier, Clemmie and I had just become parents of a baby girl, Sharleen. For the first 3 months after Sharleen's birth, Clemmie stayed home. Then, when Clemmie decided to return to work, her mother undertook to look after Sharleen, from Sunday to Friday. This led to the hectic Fridays that I will now describe.

A typical Friday went like this. From 10a.m. to 1p.m., I attended lectures in Chemistry. Then, from 2 to 5p.m., I demonstrated a lab course in Analytical Chemistry. Just after 5p.m., Clemmie met me at McGill's Roddick memorial gates. She was working at The Engineering Institute of Canada (on Mansfield Street) at the time. We climbed in to our little English car, and drove to Chambly — a southern counties village, some 20 miles south of Montreal. Sometimes we stopped briefly at the St.

Lawrence Market (enroute to Chambly), to buy meat and provisions.

Once we arrived at my in-law's home in Chambly, the routine was… ' wolf down dinner, bundle Sharleen and her belongings into our car, and drive more than 20 miles to our Côte des Neiges apartment.' We would take Sharleen upstairs to our apartment, and unpack the car. Then, I would drive (about 5 miles) back downtown to Sir George Williams, to begin lecturing at 8:25 p.m. I was scheduled to finish lecturing at 10:15 p.m. But more often than not, I continued lecturing for another 5 to 10 minutes — particularly if there was some special point that I wanted to elaborate on.

Despite the hectic schedule — and specifically the 5 to 8:25 p.m. period — I managed to get through it without undue difficulty. I am sure that I could not do it today. But I was much younger back then — 46 years younger, to be exact.

M.Sc. Graduation: (1956)

Now let us get back to discussing the steps that led ultimately to the   resumption of my PhD studies.

Initially, I thought that I would complete my Ph.D. at the University of New Brunswick, in Fredericton. I had applied and been accepted there. My plan was to leave Clemmie and our daughter in Montreal, where she could rely on support from her mother in caring for our daughter. I would commute from Fredericton from time to time, as my studies permitted. Clemmie would not hear of such a plan. If I went to Fredericton, we would all go there. Or no one would go. I chose the latter option, and took a job with a research group at Merck & Company, in Montreal.

At Merck, we were engaged in what is known euphemistically as 'custom organic synthesis'. Over the 3 years that I worked in that group, I came to understand that 'custom synthesis' (of the type that we did), meant attempting syntheses that people were willing to pay you to do, if you were foolish enough to undertake them. The procedures were often hazardous, and it was not uncommon to have to remove shards of glass from your face, as a result of exploding glassware during the synthesis. But it was only after working in this environment that I finally felt qualified enough to call myself an organic chemist.

However, for me, life as a M.Sc. chemist was far less satisfactory than what I had experienced at the B.Sc. level. Essentially, you were perceived as being a failed Ph.D. You were neither fish nor fowl. And despite having successfully completed roughly 95% of the assigned syntheses (oftentimes staying late into the night to do so), I never received a raise in the 3 years that I worked at Merck. Contrast this with my experience salary-wise at Dewy & Almy, which I related earlier.

One day, Dr. Stuart (the Director of Research at

Merck) said to me, for no apparent reason …. "Tom, you should go on for your Ph.D. That will shield you from on-the-job discrimination". Little did he know how idealistically naive his statement would prove to be.

Now, I had not abandoned the idea of continuing my graduate studies, when I took the job with Merck. Rather, I had merely postponed doing so, until our daughter (Sharleen) was old enough to be sent to a nursery school.

In July or August 1959, Clemmie contacted the owner of a nursery school by telephone. The school had been recommended to us by some of our friends. Clemmie and the proprietor (Mrs. Darling) got along so well on the telephone, that she suggested we bring Sharleen to the school before the actual opening, to get acquainted with it. So one evening, shortly after 5pm, Clemmie, Sharleen and I, drove to the nursery school. Once there, Sharleen was exuberant, as she inspected the various playthings that were available. " Look Mummy" ….she enthused, … "I will get to play on the merry-go-round, and the swings here!"

Incredulously, I heard Mrs. Darling mutter

something like …. " I don't know about that!". When asked to explain her remark, she blurted out …. "But you didn't say that you were coloured!" Clemmie responded by informing her that she had been looking for a nursery school to enroll our daughter in; she had not been looking for a nursery school for a coloured child! On hearing this exchange, I was infuriated. I informed Mrs. Darling that, given her obvious bigotry, we would never consider sending Sharleen to her school under any circumstances.

When I got home, I drafted a Letter to the Editor of the Montreal Star, detailing what had taken place. I pointed out that, at that time, I was a 'coloured' instuctor, teaching an evening class of some 75 students at 'Sir George' At best, there were no more than 3 'coloured' students in my class. Yet, when I attempted to enroll my daughter in nursery school, she was effectively denied entry, because she was coloured! Rhetorically, I asked, …. "Is this Montreal (Canada), or is this Little Rock (Arkansas)?"

From the time the Montreal Star reached the streets (around 5pm) the next day, we were inundated with telephone calls (up to about 11pm), all offering support. There were also calls from several nursery schools, offering to accept Sharleen. We chose to enroll her in a French-speaking nursery school, L' Academie Michelle Prevost

This was done in keeping with advice given by the renowned neurosurgeon, Dr. Wilder Penfield, who advised that all children should begin to learn another language at age 3. Sharleen was 4 at that time. And she was the only 'coloured' student in the nursery school.

With Sharleen finally enrolled in a French-speaking nursery school, I began to look into my return to graduate school. It turned out that I would also be enrolled at a French-speaking institution when I returned to school.

I had contacted Dr. Piché, (a professor of chemistry at l'Université de Montréal (U.de M.)), for permission to study for a Ph.D. under his supervision. He welcomed me enthusiastically, and took extraordinary steps to meld me fully into his research group there.

In 1959, I started my Ph.D. project initially under the supervision of Dr. Piché. Later I worked jointly under Drs. Piché and Berse, when Dr. Piché became Vice-Rector of the university. I will not go into details of the 3 years that I spent at U. de M., while working on my Ph.D. Suffice it to say that, in contrast to my experience at McGill, I was treated like a visiting prince at l'U. de M.. And, incredible as it may seem, this superb treatment was given to me — a black, English-speaking Protestant, at a French-speaking, Roman Catholic institution!

However, there are two memorable incidents at l'U. de M. that I want to mention. The first was when I approached Dr. Berse (in what turned out to be my final year), telling him that I had to quit school. Clemmie and Sharleen were ill, and I had no funds with which to continue my graduate studies. Dr. Berse would not hear of me quitting school. Immediately, he gave me $400 from his research funds. This was enough to pay our $75-dollars-a-month rent for more than 5 months.

The next day, the department made me an assistant professor, responsible for 30 fourth-year chemistry students. Thus all of my immediate financial needs were met, thanks to his initiatives and generosity. And I was therefore able to complete my graduate studies.

But Professor Berse was much more than my thesis-advisor. We became friends. In two successive years, he gave a magnificent Christmas party, to which he also invited Clemmie, along with some of his departmental colleagues. Subsequently, Clemmie and I reciprocated by inviting him and Mrs. Berse to our home. We kept in touch (albeit irregularly) over the years. So I was saddened to learn of his unexpected passing (on July 16, 1989), through reading his obituary in an issue of Canadian Chemical News. He was indeed a gentleman and a scholar.

The second event occurred on the day that I received my Ph.D. On October 20, 1962 Dr. Piché was presiding at the convocation exercises, in his capacity as the university Vice-Rector. As we shook hands, just as my Ph.D. epaulette was being pinned onto the left shoulder of my graduation gown, Dr. Piché said to me…. "I can think of no one that I would rather see get this degree than you!" Even 40 years later, it is still one of the nicest things that has ever been said to me.

Receiving PhD Diploma from Dr. Lucien Piche.
My Director of Research and Vice-Rector of the University
of Montreal (10/20/62)

Signing the University's Golden Book (After receiving the PhD 10/20/62)

Sharleen, Clemie and me in the University Hall of Honour
following convocation (10/20/62)

Wearing my PhD hood.

Sharleen, Sharon, Mother, Clemie and me in the Hall of
Honour (U of M) following the convocation.

Clemie, Sharleen, Sharon and Mrs. Tuitt.

That same year (1962), my younger brother Michael graduated with a B.Com. from Sir George, with a major in accountancy. I was proud and happy for him. He had done his entire post-secondary studies as an evening – division student.

CHAPTER FIVE

OUT OF THE COCOON

After being granted my Ph.D. degree, I was ready to begin my life as a research chemist, and to be gainfully employed as such, in Canada! I was about to 'try my wings' so to speak.

I had declined post-doctoral appointments both in England and in Switzerland. At 35, I thought that it was time to return to earning instead of simply to learning.

I had also changed my mind about accepting a position that I had obtained with National Distillers (in Cincinnati, Ohio). My interview went well, the starting salary was good, and they were willing to pay 75% of my relocation expenses. But in the end, I decided that I preferred to remain in Canada, provided I could find suitable work here.

When I told Dr. Piché about my decision to seek work in Canada, he made a telephone call to Dr. Roger Gaudry, the Director of Research at Ayerst Research Laboratories.

He told Dr. Gaudry that I had completed my Ph.D. program, and was looking for work in a research laboratory. Dr. Gaudry interviewed me, and then hired me as Assistant Group-Leader of the Chemical Development Group. This group was responsible for the scaling-up of products synthesized by chemists in the pure research group.

The scale-up work involved carrying out laboratory syntheses (in glass equipment up to 22 liters), followed by further scale-up in pilot-plant equipment (up to 100 gallons). Such work was intended to provide guidance for plant-scale preparation of new pharmaceutical products.

I was delighted to be asked to join such an impressive group of researchers as were present at Ayerst in 1962. The staff numbered about 250, of whom 5 were MDs, 45 had PhDs, and the preponderance of the remainder had either Masters or Bachelors degrees. A sprinkling of technicians completed the research personnel.

In addition to the excellence of the staff at Ayerst, I was also impressed with the extensive scientific literature available either in (or through) its research library. The library was headed by Dr. Carl von Seemann. Carl was an eloquent promoter of the Ayerst laboratories, although invariably he would resort to hyperbole when doing so. He also suffered from narcolepsy. Sometimes, he would fall asleep while talking to you. Or, he would fall asleep during a scientific meeting, then wake up suddenly and ask a highly relevant question — as though he had been paying attention to the proceedings all along.

One incident involving Carl still stands out in my mind. He was showing a group of Nursing students around our new pilot plant, the cost of which he inflated greatly. Later, he told them that the raw material (pregnant mare's urine;PMU) for one of Ayersts' major products Premarin was collected, over about the first two-thirds of the mare's 11 to 12-month gestation period.

One ingénue student-nurse rendered Carl speechless, by suggesting that elephant's urine should be a better source of Premarin (than PMU), because elephants have a gestation period of two years! This was the only time that I ever saw Carl unable to provide a follow-up comment.

I enjoyed my work at Ayerst, especially during my first three years there. The work was interesting and challenging. Projects involved work on such diverse pharmaceuticals as anti-depressants, anti-convulsants, steroidal oral contraceptives and serum cholesterol-lowering agents.

As part of my duties as the Assistant-Group Leader, I organized a weekly project-review session, which was open to all members of the Chemical Development Group, irrespective of whether they were graduate chemists or technicians. This was with a view to fostering (among all members of our group) a sense of them being important to the outcome of the project.

At one of these sessions, I was describing the steps that I had taken while attempting to optimize a 10-step steroid synthesis that I had been working on. The synthesis had been sent to our group (by 'pure research') for optimization and eventual scale-up in our Pilot Plant.

After my detailed presentation, a technician asked…. "Why didn't you carry out the Grignard reaction at step 2 of the synthesis?" Astounded (by the astuteness of the question), I exclaimed almost involuntarily … " My God! It never occurred to me to do so!"

I did as the technician had suggested. The result was that I was able to eliminate five steps from the synthesis, and double the yield of product.

From that time on, in all my endeavours, I have sought and accepted good advice from wherever it is available.

Shortly after the end of my third year at Ayerst, my idyllic involvement there took an unexpected adverse turn. Prior to then, I had received a salary increase every time one was due. In fact, sometime in April or May that year, I received a call from Dr. Gaudry, asking me to come to his office. When I got there he said to me … "Dr. Massiah, I am very pleased with your work, and I have decided to reward you with double the usual annual increase (in June), instead of December!" I thanked him, and left his office in a buoyant mood. Shortly after that, Dr. Gaudry left Ayerst, to become the Rector of l'Université de Montréal.

When I got home that evening, I told Clemmie what had transpired, and together we looked forward to June, when I would receive my substantial salary-increase. June came, but there was no increase in my salary. So I called the Associate-Director of Research, Dr. Glen — who had not hired me, but to whom I reported ultimately — asking him about the raise that Dr. Gaudry had promised me. I will not go into details of my conversation with Dr. Glen, except to say that I emerged from his office with a clear understanding that I had no future at Ayerst. The probable underlying reasons are almost too embarrassing, even to speculate about.

It seems that unofficially, there was a 'Gaudry' faction and a 'Glen' faction at Ayerst. I found myself part of the 'Gaudry' faction (since it was he who had hired me), yet I reported to Dr. Glen. However, despite my misaligned allegiance, at no time did I make this dichotomy obvious to Dr. Glen. So the reason for the antagonism that he exhibited towards me during my salary inquiry (after Dr. Gaudry had left Ayerst) remains unclear.

In any event, it was time to move on. Therefore, I applied for (and obtained) a position as Group-Leader Chemical-Development, at Canada Packers in Toronto. Before I left Ayerst, I made a determined effort to finish any outstanding projects, and also to write especially detailed final reports.

To my complete surprise, the Christmas after I left Ayerst, I received a gigantic card (from Ayerst) signed 'Bill Glen'.

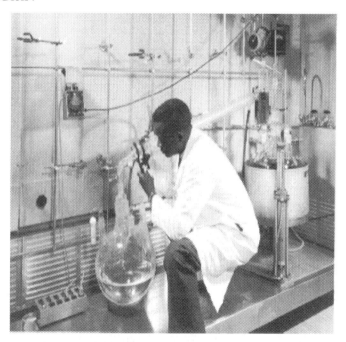

Me, in the Pilot Plant laboratory fume hood, at Ayerst Research Laboratories: Montreal: (1962)

CHAPTER SIX

ON EAGLE'S WINGS!

The 18-year period (1966-1984) was a time of significant growth, in both my professional and personal life. Like Phoenix (of Egyptian mythology), I had risen from the ashes of many tribulations, 'to soar on eagle's wings' so to speak. I will elaborate.

In April 1966, I was moved to Toronto (by Canada Packers Limited) to join the Research Department, as Group-Leader of Chemical Development. Professionally, I was not only a research chemist, but was now also a department head. And my biography had just been published in American Men of Science, later re-named American Men & Women of Science. I had indeed come a long way from Lacasse Street, in Montreal's St. Henri district. I was proud — but not prideful.

In my office at Canada Packers Research Centre:

(1966)

At the time that I joined Canada Packers, the Research Centre had just been refurbished and expanded. The staff numbered roughly 80 — some 10 of who had a Ph.D. degree. I had a staff of five. In addition, I was responsible for the running of a Pilot Plant and two laboratories. At first, I was rather dismayed with the Pilot Plant, which looked primitive in comparison to the one at Ayerst. However, it worked surprisingly well, especially after I had improvements made by the Canada Packers maintenance department.

On taking up my new position, I decided that I would try to apply three important lessons that I learned over my many years as a chemist, in my operational style.

➢ The first lesson was, the need to instill a sense within my collaborators, that they were vital to the success of any research projects undertaken by the group. It is also important that each participant be given a clear understanding of where the particular project (with which he or she is involved), fits into the overall research objectives. In other words, why are we working on this project, and why is it important?

➢ The second important lesson is embodied in the truism that 'a well-defined problem is already half solved!' I had read that statement shortly before I joined Canada Packers, and I had it displayed prominently on my office wall thereafter. I urged my staff to adopt it as their credo, when embarking on a research project.

➢ The third and final lesson that I tried to impart to my

collaborators was that 'similar things occur to similar people' Expanded, this simply means that if similarly trained people all start to solve the same problem, from the same perspective, it is unreasonable to expect that a unique solution will emerge.

Therefore, in order to come up with a unique solution, it is mandatory for one to perambulate mentally about the problem, so as to avail yourself of many additional perspectives.

Earlier, I mentioned how I had used essentially the latter two lessons, to conclude my M.Sc. work at McGill. And, as I will show later in this memoir (in summarizing my achievements), I invoked them repeatedly throughout my 18 year tenure at Canada Packers, to solve many difficult technical problems.

One major difference that I noticed when I joined Canada Packers, was how research work was instituted there, as compared to how it was done at Ayerst. Before any research project was started at Canada Packers, a detailed cost-estimate had to be done. The wisdom of doing so became immediately obvious, since it would be pointless to develop a procedure (costing say $500/kg.), to prepare a product that would sell for $200/kg. Such was not the case at Ayerst. There, research was conducted much more liberally, and seemingly without the cost restraints that detailed cost-estimates would impose. Perhaps this was due to the greater research funding available in the pricey pharmaceutical environment, compared to that of a packinghouse, such as at Canada Packers. Now, what about the projects tackled by my group?

As things would have it, the first project that I undertook at Canada Packers, was the isolation of an amino acid (L-cystine) from chicken feathers. This was somewhat fortuitous, in that I had extensive experience with this amino acid, having worked with it during my Ph.D. project at l'U. de M. L- Cystine (specifically in its reduced form, L-cysteine) was needed in both the bread-making and pharmaceutical industries. It is obtainable from a class of proteins known as keratins. Human hair, hog hair and chicken feathers are examples of keratins. Since the latter two substances were readily available from the Canada Packers abattoir, they were the first raw materials that we investigated.

There is an interesting aside, with respect to our use of chicken feathers, as a source of L-cystine. Prior to the Chemical Development Group expressing an interest in chicken feathers as a raw material, the Canada Packers plant operatives were paying $20 a truckload to have them disposed of. However, once our interest became known, they charged us $8/ton for it, even though we were part of the same organization. This was in keeping with Canada Packers' 'no internal subsidy policy' that existed at that time.

We were able to isolate high-purity L-Cystine from a number of keratins such as chicken feathers and human hair — especially that from India and China. This was achieved by a procedure that I devised, which exploited the uniqueness of cystine's structure, among the 26 or so known amino acids. But we were never able to develop a procedure that was either technically or economically feasible. So we abandoned further isolation work on this product, since it was more readily available from fermentation.

I am going to digress from discussing my work at

Canada Packers (for the time being), in order to provide an overview of a number of developments in my life, that were taking place concurrently.

For one thing, after moving to Toronto, I began to write a letter to Mother, each week, letting her know how things were going for us. One week, I did not write to her (because Clemmie had taken ill), and I didn't want to let her know about it.   Mother called sometime during the next week, saying ---- " I did not get your letter last week!" I had not realized that she looked forward to getting a letter from me each week.

My letters continued from April until early December 1966, when I was told that Mother was seriously ill, and had been hospitalized. It was shortly before Christmas. Clemmie, Sharleen and I drove down to Montreal to see Mother. When we got to the hospital, it became apparent immediately that she was dying. We stayed for some three or four days, then I had to return to Toronto, because I had not applied for compassionate leave initially. But I knew that we would be returning to Montreal soon.

About 1a.m. (on January 01, 1967), I received a

telephone call from Montreal telling me that Mother had passed away. It was the start of Canada's Centennial Year! Mother was 67.

I drove down to Montreal at a snail's pace, trying to come to terms with my loss. Clemmie was a tower of strength for me in this traumatic situation.

Mother was cremated, in accordance with a wish that she had expressed many times. And her ashes were spread to 'the four corners of the wind', again according to her wishes. Only my younger brother, Michael and I (who did the actual spreading of her ashes) know the location. She had had a very arduous life. She was now at rest.

In 1968, I became the second President of a club called the University Negro Alumni Club (UNAC). This group was somewhat similar to the group (MNAG) that I had founded back in 1953, but was more socially oriented (and less involved with education), than was the MNAG. In fact, this was my major disappointment with UNAC. Our social life was greatly enhanced, by being members of it. But despite the calibre of the membership, they resisted any attempts I made to get them involved with social activism, on behalf of the black community. I served a two-year term as President. UNAC was disbanded some five years later.

1972 heralded the start of two significant involvements for me. The first was becoming the spokesman on police-community relations, on behalf of the National Black Coalition (NBC). The second was that I joined the Association of the Chemical Profession of Ontario (ACPO). Briefly, here are the details.

My police-community work, on behalf of the NBC, came about accidentally. I had been invited to attend a meeting between the police and members of the black community, at Neighbourhood House, on Bathurst Street.

There was a great deal of anger being directed at the police, over allegations of police brutality. The Deputy-Chief Jack Ackroyd asked us to introduce ourselves. I got up and said …. "My name is Tom Massiah. I have come here to listen, to learn, and hopefully to contribute." Then I sat down.

Subsequent to the meeting, Inspector Jack Marks (who had accompanied Deputy-Chief Akroyd to the meeting), asked Kay Livingstone if I would be willing to give a talk on police-community relations, at the Police College, situated on Willowdale Avenue. Even though my expertise was in the field of science, rather than sociology, I felt duty-bound nevertheless to accept the challenge. So I chose Arthur Downes and Sheldon Taylor to accompany me for the talks to the police, as they had been involved in community affairs for some time.

The talks presented were: -

➢ THE VISIBLE MINORITY: May 14, 1972

➢ THE DEVELOPMENT OF ATTITUDES ABOUT THE VISIBLE MINORITY: June 20, 1972

➢ A BRIEF PRESENTED TO THE TASK FORCE ON POLICING IN ONTARIO: April 04, 1973

➢ THE ROLE OF THE POLICE IN THE COMMUNITY: February 24, 1975

While the presentations were received politely, absolutely nothing changed in how members of the Black community were being treated by the Toronto police. Nor has anything of substance happened up till now.

The police continue to deny that racism exists in police practices. And until they stop the denials, nothing will change. I feel that this is still true in 2001.

Arthur Downes and Sheldon Taylor were very

helpful in conveying the Black community's concerns about policing in Toronto, while serving on our 3-man delegation.

Subsequently, Arthur became a Justice of the Peace, and served as such until he retired. Sheldon earned a Ph.D. in History at the U. of T.(1994). Both he and Arthur continue to be active in community affairs, on behalf of Toronto's Black citizens.

As I said earlier, in 1972, I became a member of the Association of the Chemical Profession of Ontario (ACPO). Shortly after joining the ACPO, I was elected a councillor for one of the Toronto districts. Then I became Chairman of the ACPO Professional Affairs Committee, a position that I held for 3 years (1974-1977). I became Vice-President in 1978. From 1979 to 1981, I served as the President of the ACPO. My final office with the ACPO was as Past President, 1981-1983.

During my tenure as President, I led the ACPO's efforts to obtain Licensure for chemists in Ontario. To date, the Ontario government has resisted every attempt by the ACPO for licensing Ontario's chemists — something that Quebec chemists were granted more than 30 years ago. Instead, in 1985, the Ontario government granted us the almost meaningless designation of Chartered Chemist (C.Chem.).

In leading the ACPO's quest for the licensure of Ontario's chemists, I was not motivated by a selfish desire to aggrandize either chemistry or its practitioners. Rather it was because I wanted to ensure that Chemistry (sometimes called the Central Science) was practiced only by competent practitioners, in the public interest. Politicians (the preponderance of whom are lawyers) never seem to be able to grasp how pervasive Chemistry is, in our day-to-day lives. They seem to believe that Chemistry can be done by anyone! Perhaps that explains why the cleanup of the gigantic 1979 chemical spill (in Mississauga, ON), was done under the supervision of the then Ontario Attorney-General!

So now, let us return to discussing my research work at Canada Packers. In 1972, my group became involved with a major pharmaceutical project in collaboration with the Cedars-Sinai hospital in Los Angeles, CA. The product, Chenodeoxycholic Acid (or CDCA), had shown that it could dissolve certain types of cholesterol-containing gallstones, thus obviating the need for gallbladder surgery.

It is a naturally occurring bile acid that had been isolated previously, in laboratory-scale amounts, from hog bile. Our challenge was to develop a procedure for isolating it in pharmaceutical purity and plant-size amounts. I will skip all but the absolutely essential details, in reporting how we fared with this project.

We succeeded in developing and patenting a procedure for isolating high-purity CDCA from hog bile. But while in effect we had won the battle, we would eventually lose the war! I will explain. There were two crucial pieces of advice about this project, that I had given my immediate superior (at Canada Packers), which were ignored. The first had to do with a product specification, and the other concerned the raw material source.

I had recommended that we should not list a melting point in the specifications for our product. The reason was that I thought that the melting point of our product was too diffuse to be used as a criterion of purity. Pure, crystalline products always have sharp, narrow-range melting points! Yet, despite my recommendation, a melting point was listed in the specifications. This was one of two factors that made our product unacceptable ultimately, after some 8 years of research. A competitor had prepared a product that had a substantially higher, sharp melting point, that was deemed to be preferable to our product. And it was synthesized from cholic acid — an alternative raw material that I had recommended that we consider, concurrent with our development work, using hog bile. My recommendation regarding the use of cholic acid (to prepare chenodeoxycholic acid) was particularly germane, since Canada Packers had considerable expertise in preparing this acid from beef bile. But my recommendation was ignored. In my opinion, we would have succeeded in bringing CDCA to the marketplace, had my recommendations about it been accepted.

Another major project that floundered (due to unheeded advice from me) involved the antibiotics, semi-synthetic penicillins. However, I must provide a small amount of background information, in order to make the critical issues clearer.

For this purpose, I will represent natural penicillin by the symbol P-X, and the various semi-synthetic penicillins, symbolically as A-X, B-X, C-X and so on, where A, B , C are different molecular moieties chemically linked to –X, a structure which is common to all penicillins. Unfortunately for lay people, -X has the intimidating name 6-aminopenicillanic acid (or simply 6-APA).

While I was still at Ayerst (and before joining Canada Packers), I met two scientists from the Beecham Research Laboratories, in the UK. They told me that Beecham was preparing 6-APA (for use in semi-synthetic penicillins) by fermentation. This was substantially cheaper than preparing it by chemically cleaving natural penicillin (i.e. P-X →P- + -X).

I had conveyed this information to my immediate superior at Canada Packers, when we embarked on the semi-synthetic penicillin project. Nevertheless, I was told to start our development work by chemically cleaving natural penicillin to obtain 6-APA.

Later, (and after our in-house fermentation group had been disbanded), 6-APA became commercially available. Thereafter, I used it to develop several plant-scale procedures for preparing high quality semi-synthetic penicillins such as ampicillin, amoxicillin and cloxacillin. We collaborated with an Italian pharmaceutical company Prodotti Terapeutici S.p.A. (PRO-TER), situated in Milan, in scaling up the procedures developed by my group. In 1975, I spent 11 days in Milan, familiarizing myself with various aspects of the scaled-up procedures. I found our Italian collaborators to be extremely good at adapting technology. And they were easily among the most hospitable and erudite people that I have encountered in my professional life.

As an aside, I will add that, during my consulting trip to Milan, I took advantage of its proximity, to spend a weekend visiting Venice. Then, enroute home to Toronto, I made a side trip to Paris, where I spent three days, exploring its sights.

However, despite our technical success with this project, eventually we were unable to compete economically, since we were **purchasers** rather than **producers** of 6-APA! The cost of that commodity determined who survived in the market. I had warned of this threat in a seminar that I gave at Canada Packers.

I think that it was sometime in 1979, that the Director of Research, Dr. Leon Rubin retired. He left to become an emeritus research professor at the University of Toronto. During the next year, Henry Nordin, one of my

Group-Leader colleagues functioned as the Acting Research Director. There was also a change in the corporate senior management. Mr. Val Stock became the company President and CEO. That year, I received an unheard of 17% salary increase. But it was the last salary increase that I would receive at Canada Packers.

The search for a new Director of Research, resulted in Dr. Bern Schnyder being hired to fill the position. From the time we first met, I sensed that there was trouble ahead for me. My apprehensions proved valid, in that I found that my administrative functions began to diminish noticeably. The situation was made worse by an ambiguous performance review given me by my immediate superior. It said in part …. *"Tom is respected by his staff. But he tends to over-control them."*

Now clearly there is something illogical in the foregoing statement. I cannot see how I could have the respect of my staff, if I over-controlled them! And it would be entirely contrary to one of the guiding principles that I enunciated earlier, regarding my operating style — namely, that of according dignity to each of my collaborators; also to make each feel vital to the success of the project in which he or she was involved.

Nevertheless, the die had been cast. At roughly 2p.m., on February 2nd, 1984 I received a telephone call from Bern, asking me to come to his office. I thought that it was to discuss some of my group's projects, so I gathered up several of the most relevant files. When I arrived in his office, he was pacing up and down, as though he was walking on hot coals. He asked me to close the door, which I did. The next thing I heard (which shocked my unbelieving ears) was something like this. "We have sold the pharmaceutical division, and are offering you early retirement, effective immediately. You do not have to do any more work for us. And you may keep your office for the next three months." He was about to list all the out-placement benefits available to me, but I interrupted his presentation, gathered up my files and said to him …. "You have made your decision, now I will make mine. My severance takes place now! I have to get on with the rest of my life."

I left his office, and went to tell my group what had happened. They were shocked! I told them that I would be back in a week to clear out my desk.

Then I left. I was 57. Seemingly I had been **LIFO'd (Last In, First Out!)** —— something well known among blacks who held other than menial jobs. But I never adopted the stance of a victim. Nor did I waste time being angry or feeling sorry for myself. It was time to move on. It was time for surmounting my next hurdle.

However, before turning to the next phase of my life, I feel impelled to summarize the achievements of my group in my 18 years at Canada Packers. They are: -

➢ Developed a commercial procedure for preparing two semi-synthetic broad-spectrum antibiotics, Ampicillin and Amoxicillin.

➢ Developed a novel commercial process for preparing Isopropyl Myristate and Palmitate, two emollients used in the cosmetic industry.

➢ Conceived and implemented an improved procedure for isolating Beef-liver Catalase, a hydrogen-peroxidase.

➢ Directed a novel process for isolating Protamine Sulfate, a Heparin antagonist, important in open-heart surgery.

> Invented and patented an industrial-scale process for preparing Choline Chloride, 80%, a non-hygroscopic form of this nutritional supplement.

> Developed and patented several processes for isolating CDCA from hog bile.

> Developed a convenient procedure for preparing fatty- acid-poor Bovine Serum Albumin, a substance of potential use in biotechnology.

> Was named as an inventor in seven patents issued to Canada Packers.

> Wrote a comprehensive survey report on Affinity Chromatography, a procedure used extensively for isolating and purifying biochemical and pharmaceutical products.

Within two years of my departure from Canada Packers, the entire Research Centre and staff had been disbanded.

I would be remiss, however, if I did not acknowledge the very comprehensive severance package that Canada Packers provided me with.

The outplacement firm, Murray Axmith &

Associates, had excellent facilities. They provide offices, in which you could work on such matters as drafting résumés, and also research possible employment leads. You could draft as many different kinds of résumés as you wished, and obtain as many copies as you wanted. Under their guidance, I became quite adept at preparing so-called 'broadcast letters', which focused the salient aspects of your training and experience much better than a typical résumé.

The other important component of the Canada Packers package was financial planning. I was put in touch with a financial planner, who (though he was paid by Canada Packers) operated 'at arms length' from them. He connected me with very competent people at Royal Trust, who advised me expertly on how to invest my severance funds. This started me on the road to the financial stability that I enjoy today.

So while there were some stultifying experiences during my years at Canada Packers, I have only good thoughts about how I was treated, on leaving their employ.

Some people have devastating memories from being early retired. But for me, in retrospect, it turned out to be the best thing that happened, during my working life up to then.

Before going on with the next phase of my life story, I want to comment on something important, that took place in 1975. That year, Clemmie and I bought a condominium, in the Royalcrest complex, situated at the northeast corner of Finch and Pharmacy avenues. It is the first and only real estate that we own. Prior to then, we were so busy with my perambulations in and out of school, that we never got around to buying any real property. We still live there.

I have been so busy chronicling events in my life that I almost forgot to mention two very important events in our family's life. Both took place in 1978.

The first was that our daughter Sharleen graduated from the University of Toronto, with an honours B.A. in psychology. Subsequently, she went on to obtain a B.S.W. (in 1982), and a M.S.W. (in 1990), both from York University. She works as an independent Social Work practitioner, for the York region, specializing in seniors' disabilities and acquired brain-injury work.

The other important event was Sharleen's marriage (on July 7) to Emeka Nwakwesi, a Nigerian, whom she had met at the U. of T. They were married in Trinity Chapel of the University of Toronto.

There were 250 friends and guests in attendance at the reception, which was held in the Make - Believe-Ballroom of Fantasy Farm.

Now to get on with the rest of my story.

CHAPTER SEVEN

THE SEVENTH AGE

In Shakespeare's 'As You Like It', the seventh (and last) stage of life is described as … *"….second childishness and mere oblivion. Sans teeth, sans eyes, sans taste, sans everything."*

Well, my seventh stage of life (which covers the years 1984- 2001), was very unlike that described by Shakespeare. Instead, they were years of even further diversified professional growth. I would embark on two new careers —— one as a consultant, and the other as a community college faculty member. But before making these two seminal career changes, I had to go through a period of introspection and re-evaluation, following my sudden unexpected separation from Canada Packers, in February 1984.

One thought that I had to establish clearly in my

mind was that what I did for a living, did not define me as an individual. Put another way, self-respect is by definition something that no one can give you. Therefore, you should not allow anyone to take that away from you.

So, it did not matter that I was no longer a Group-Leader at Canada Packers. Nor did it matter that, at that time, I was employed in the business of finding employment. But what did I want to do? Or perhaps more importantly, what did I not want to do?

After considering various options, I decided to try consulting. This seemed a perfect fit for me, given my age and extensive process-development experience. And it would give me independence — something I craved, after my strictured years in industry.

Although I was well equipped technically to offer 'hands on' consulting expertise, getting started as a consultant proved to be difficult. Something that I had not anticipated, was resistance from in-house personnel, who often regard outside consultants as a threat. Some even held the pejorative view, that a consultant was someone who borrowed your watch, in order to tell you the time!

Then there was the need to make many 'cold calls'

on potential clients — something I had never done before. But perhaps the worst thing was having to rebound from the disappointment of broken promises, from seemingly promising leads. But I had made the choice — I would become a consultant. So I persisted.

Success came in June 1984, when I was offered a consulting assignment, by Organon Canada Limited — a name-brand pharmaceutical firm, located in the Toronto suburb, West Hill. I was retained by Organon to develop a manufacturing process for preparing COTAZYM ECS®, a product used to treat cystic fibrosis. It is supplied as enteric-coated microspheres (ECS), contained in gelatin capsules.

At that time, the Organon plant in West Orange, NJ supplied the needs of the Canadian market, but it did so sporadically. However, this arrangement proved to be unsuitable. So Organon Canada Limited decided to see if it could develop in-house capability to manufacture COTAYZM ECS®. That is where I came in as the consultant.

I accepted the challenge posed by the project, even though I had never done anything quite like it before. In fact, my daughter Sharleen asked me if I thought that I could do it. I told her that I would not have accepted the assignment, if I thought that I could not do it.

The first difficulty I experienced was that, (unlike Ayerst or Canada Packers), Organon did not have either a development lab or a pilot plant, in which to develop a prototype of the preparative procedure. In fact, I did not even have a laboratory in which to work. Instead, I was given some makeshift space in an unused processing area of the Organon plant. Even such basic laboratory equipment as a water-aspirator (for use in filtering solutions), was unavailable in that area of the plant.

The absence of actual development facilities, necessitated that I use the actual process facility — a 1-meter diameter centrifugal granulator — to carry out the development work. Of course, I could not use the actual raw materials for this purpose. Nor could I prepare full-scale batches in the exploratory trials. Both of these alternatives would have been prohibitively expensive, and also inexcusably wasteful. Instead, I had to devise the minimum amount of alternative substances (other than the actual ingredients for COTAZYM ECS), to use in the process-simulation work.

Enduring confidentiality agreements prohibit me from revealing any details about the approach that I took. But I can report that I succeeded in developing a manufacturing process for preparing U.S.P.-grade COTAZYM ECS®. Moreover, the preparative cost was 50% that of purchasing the product from Organon Inc. I also provided Organon with a computer-based program (developed by Sulo Krisnamurthy, of Organon Canada Ltd.) for optimum batch blending. And I provided Organon with an optimized process flowsheet, to facilitate the batch-to-batch production. All in all, a most successful consultancy!

Throughout, I was most ably assisted by Doug Harrison, a Chemical Technology graduate of Centennial College (in Scarborough, ON).

Early in 1985, I formalized my consulting operations, by incorporating as INNOCHEM CONSULTANTS LIMITED. I incorporated in order to reduce personal liability for any consulting advice that I may have given, in the course of performing my consulting activities. My aim was to specialize in developing processes for manufacturing pharmaceutical products. This would include both known pharmaceuticals, as well as newly conceptualized improvements to existing pharmaceuticals.

I operated out of a home office. In this way, I could minimize my operating costs while attempting to establish my consulting business. My wife, Clemmie was listed as the Secretary- Treasurer, and I was listed as the President. So effectively, it was a one-man two person corporation. However, I had tacit agreements with a number of professionals, whom I could access on an 'ad hoc' basis.

I continued to make 'cold calls', and to send out unsolicited proposals to target firms. The proposals were of the type known as 'Intellectual Property'. What I proposed, was to develop novel pharmaceutical products (which I had conceptualized), in collaboration with the client firm. I focused on semi-synthetic penicillins, since to me, they offered the greatest potential for commercial exploitation.

After receiving several turndowns from prominent pharmaceutical firms, I received a very non-committal kind of proposal from the Eli Lilly Research Laboratories, in Indianapolis. I rejected their proposal, and submitted a counterproposal, in which I presented my unalterable conditions for continuing the venture. This proved to be successful. I was invited to the Lilly research campus, for a one-day consultancy, to present my proposal.

On August 14, 1985 I flew to Indianapolis and checked in to the hotel that had been reserved for me. After dinner, I spent the rest of the evening rehearsing my presentation. Then I turned in, determined to get a good night's sleep, in preparation for the next day's activities.

Shortly after 8a.m. the next day, Dr. Patrick Roffey, a Vice-President of Research, picked me up at the hotel. Then it was off to the Lilly Research campus. What a sight awaited me. It was huge. Forty-four (i.e. eleven by four) city blocks in total. A still greater surprise, was the size of the research staff. They numbered 2500, with 500 Ph.Ds.; each in their own lab, and each was assisted usually by an M.Sc. scientist. But my greatest surprise came when I was introduced to the first scientist in the group that was to hear and question me on my presentation. He was someone whose many publications (in the field of semi-synthetic penicillins) I had read over the years. What could I tell him?

Well I had no choice but to give it my best shot. So I forgot about how intimidated I should have felt, and launched into my presentation. It went very well. After some 90 minutes, which included time for questions, I felt that I had made a good impression on my audience. Based on their post-presentation questions, and the extensive openness shown me afterwards, I felt assured that I had ignited their interest in my proposals.

What I had discussed were five semi-synthetic penicillins (that I had conceptualized), which should be resistant to substances known as ß-lactamases. These are substances (produced by certain bacteria), which are capable of inactivating penicillins. However, if the penicillin is ß-lactamase-resistant, then it would be effective against ß-lactamase producing bacteria.

The Lilly people did a thorough computerized search of the compounds that I had proposed. They determined that indeed three were novel. So they decided to consider the three novel compounds, to see if they should begin work on them. I had hoped that they would do so, since I had negotiated a generous royalty agreement with them. They would deliberate about this for another three months. But in the end, they decided to investigate monoclonal antibodies, (rather than my proposed compounds), because they provided a better fit with their corporate objectives. Close, but no cigar! I was disappointed, but I had to accept Lilly's priority-based decision.

After my encounter with Eli Lilly and Company, I continued my efforts to obtain consulting work, from both large and small firms. But aside from several follow-up consultancies at Organon, assignments continued to be sporadic. However, these were insufficient to rely on solely for my livelihood. So, in 1985, when I was offered a part-time teaching assignment in the Biological, Pharmaceutical and Chemical Technology Department of Seneca College, I accepted. This would provide a steady (albeit modest) income, while I continued my search for consulting clients.

I found the teaching assignment to be surprisingly enjoyable. So after my initial assignment was over, I signed on with Seneca for another one semester, as a partial-load faculty member. Under this arrangement, you are paid on an hourly basis, and there are no employee benefits. Again, I found the teaching to be enjoyable. Therefore, at the end of that semester, I applied for a full-time faculty position at the Newnham Campus of Seneca College. I was accepted, beginning in January 1986. My pay was about double what I had received as a partial-load faculty member. And I received all of the very generous benefits available at Seneca. For the first time since February 1984, I had a steady and substantial income. This would permit me to search for consulting assignments more leisurely.

Shortly after signing on as a full-time faculty member at Seneca, I received a very pleasant surprise. Due to the diligence of my friend Romain Pitt (now Mr. Justice Pitt of the Superior Court of Justice (Ont.)), I was appointed to the position of a member of the **Drug Quality and Therapeutics Committee (DQTC).**

This is an advisory board, appointed by the Lieutenant - Governor, through an Order-in-Council, to advise the Ontario Ministry of Health, about which drugs to list in its Formulary. It numbers about 20 members, and consists of medical specialists, pharmacists, statisticians, pharmaceutical and biological chemists and some external consultants, who could be accessed on an 'ad hoc' basis. My initial appointment was for a one-year term, effective January 24, 1986. I was re-appointed in each of the next two years. So overall, I served on the DQTC for three years.

I found it extremely stimulating to be a member of the DQTC. The things that we were asked to decide were momentous, both in terms of the drug costs and health implications for Ontario's citizens. The way the committee functioned was like this. When the documents required by the Ministry of Health were received from the firm that wanted its product listed in the Formulary, these documents were assigned to appropriate members of the DQTC. The member (or members) would prepare a report on the product(s) that were seeking to be listed in the Formulary. The report(s) were then circulated to the entire committee, for study, prior to the meeting at which the findings on the product would be discussed. If the product met the criteria established for being listed in the Formulary, the petitioner was so advised by the Ministry. Otherwise, the petitioner was told what was defective in the documentation, and advised that the product would not be listed in the Formulary.

The appointment to the DQTC was indeed an epochal event for me. Not only was I earning a good salary at Seneca, but I was also involved in challenging, highly remunerative consulting work, as a committee member.

Happily, I was able to arrange my schedule at Seneca so that it did not interfere with my DQTC work. I will have more to say about the DQTC later.

Now for some specifics about my five years as a full-time Seneca faculty member.

When I joined Seneca, several people (including students) asked me why I had not opted to teach at university. After all, I had both the academic qualifications and experience to do so. In fact, I had also received 'feelers' from someone connected with York University, inviting me to apply for a position there. I decided not to do so for two reasons. First, I was not interested in getting involved with 'university politics' at this age and stage of my life. The minimum rank that I would accept at a university would be Associate Professor, and I was not prepared to even consider a lower rank. Second, my brief teaching stints at Seneca, convinced me that that was where I could be of greatest benefit to the students. My many years of practical, 'hands on' experience, was ideally suited to the needs of community college students, such as those at Seneca. I was not interested in establishing a landmark career at Seneca. I just wanted to be an effective teacher.

The faculty at Seneca was unionized — something that I always thought to be out of place in an academic environment. So I never signed a union card, event though there was a mandatory union-dues check off.

Within weeks of joining Seneca full-time, the union called what I considered to be an ill-considered strike, based on receiving a 51% affirmative vote from the faculty. Just before doing so however, they had rejected a 6% salary increase, offered by the College's Board of Regents.

I apologized to my classes, telling them that, while I disagreed completely with the strike, I would not attempt to cross the picket lines. This is because striking faculty were harassing any non-striking faculty who attempted to cross the picket lines. But I also assured them that I would not be drawing strike pay. For the duration of the strike, I would forfeit my entire salary.

My daughter Sharleen questioned the wisdom of this decision, and urged me to reconsider it. I told her that I had to look at myself in the mirror, every day when I shaved. How could I say that I opposed the strike, and yet accept strike pay? My principles were not for sale!

After 6 weeks, the strike was settled. What was

gained? In my view, absolutely nothing. The union settled for the 6% salary increase that had been offered initially. So the strike was clearly shown to have been unnecessary. And the biggest 'gain' was that thereafter, all faculty could use the hitherto esteemed title 'Professor'. I thought that this wanton grant of such a prestigious title was completely irresponsible. The title 'Professor' belongs exclusively in a university, and is only bestowed on properly qualified persons, usually after a minimum of 7 years of demonstrated teaching competence.

Very few of the faculty at Seneca, could meet this minimum criterion. Besides, Seneca is a Community College! It is not a university.

Although I had both the academic qualifications (and 15 years of university-level teaching experience), I declined using the title 'Professor'. Instead, I simply signed 'Instructor' when needed, on official college documents.

After the strike was over, I resumed my teaching duties. At Seneca, your teaching course load was listed on what was called a Standard Work Form (SWF). Whenever my SWF was presented, I simply asked, where do I sign? However, those of my colleagues who were union adherents often instituted grievance proceedings, over some aspect of the SWF with which they disagreed. I didn't have time for that, since for the most part I did not find the workload to be unreasonable, especially in comparison to what I had done out in the work-a-day world.

Initially, I was assigned to teach courses in General Chemistry, Introductory Organic chemistry and Pharmaceutical Science. Each of these courses had both a lecture and a laboratory component. So each week, I had to mark something like 100 lab reports. This necessitated that I institute inviolable rules, as to when reports were to be received, and how they were to be presented. There was no discussion of alternative procedures. Otherwise, there would be no way for me to keep up with the marking. I had no problem with the students, once I made it clear as to what was the operative system.

Since Seneca is an institution where the teaching of technology skills is emphasized, I took special pleasure in the pre-lab discussion that I gave. In it, I would give a detailed explanation of the purpose(s) of the experiment, the chemistry involved, and the method of reporting the observed results. Throughout, my discussion focused on 'how to' (i.e. practice or practical), rather than 'why' (i.e. theory or theoretical).

Subsequently, I was assigned to teach several technical mathematics courses, when I expressed surprise (at a faculty meeting), that students had difficulty understanding mathematics. I was pleased with this development, since mathematics is a hobby of mine. Besides, I found teaching mathematics to be easier, than teaching a course in General Chemistry. So, from then until the end of my full-time teaching at Seneca, I taught Technical Mathematics, Introductory and Advanced Organic Chemistry, and Pharmaceutical Science.

One thing that never ceased to amaze me when I taught mathematics, was how blissfully students ignored the difference between a plus (+) and a minus(−) sign. For example, they would work out a problem using a mathematical device known as a determinant. Let us say that the numerical answer should have a positive (+) sign. The student would report the correct numerical answer, but assign a negative (−) sign to it. When I would mark the answer as being incorrect, the usual response was … "Sir, may I have part marks for my answer?" My response went like this. "Mr. X, if your friendly banker told you that your bank balance was −$3000, would you think that you had $3000 in your account? Or if you went to a surgeon for a gallbladder operation, and he amputated your leg, would you pay him part fees?"

But no matter how many analogies I presented, plus (+) and minus (−) signs remained interchangeable to many of my mathematics students.

Teaching was not my only involvement at Seneca. In 1988, I agreed to be Co-Chairman for a scientific meeting, known by the acronym 2YC/3C. This meeting involved 2-year junior colleges in the U.S., and 3-year community colleges in Canada. The overall Chairman was Dr. Murray Morello, a colleague at Seneca. Together (with my opposite number in the U.S.), we organized a 3-day Seneca-based conference, at which there were some 250 registrants. The scientific papers presented were of surprisingly good quality.

We also organized several attractive leisure activities for the registrants. An elegant dinner, at the Ontario Science Centre capped off the conference. Overall, it was a most successful undertaking.

Another non-teaching involvement, while I was at Seneca, took place on August 14, 1989, when I agreed to give a talk at Queens University, as part of the CHEMED program being held there. In my talk, I proposed that Community Colleges should stick to their original mission — that of teaching applied technology — rather than trying to become quasi-universities. I still hold to that view today, although the trend seems to be going in the opposite direction.

There has been a proliferation of merges of Community Colleges with Universities (such as Seneca with York University for example), as well as former technological institutions morphing into universities, such as happened with Ryerson Polytechnic Institute.

For the next 2 years, my teaching activities at Seneca continued more or less uneventfully. But exactly 6 months before my 65th birthday, I received a call from the Human Resources department, informing me that I would be retiring on August 30, 1991 — 4 days after my birthday. Talk about early retirement! In any event, I began immediately to look into matters pertaining to my pension. I asked the Human Resources department if it would be possible to 'buy back' my part-time at Seneca, so as to have it counted as full-time on my pension. It was. So I forwarded the required amount to the pension department, and the adjustment was made to my full-time credit. I am happy that I took this step, because it did not take much time for me to recoup the money that I had paid out, once I actually became a pensioner.

I was given a very nice send-off by my colleagues, once my actual retirement date rolled around. The send-off included a luncheon (which Clemmie also attended), at which I was given a personal organizer, as a gift.

For nearly 5 years, after retiring from the full-time faculty, I taught in the continuing education department at Seneca, two evenings a week. I taught primarily both introductory and advanced Technical Mathematics courses.

One drawback to teaching in the continuing education department, was that I went from top salary in the full-time teaching, to bottom salary in the evening division teaching. But during one Summer session, I was asked to teach a course on Business Communications — a course that I greatly enjoyed teaching. However, in 1995, I decided to discontinue teaching in Seneca's continuing education department. I no longer found it satisfying to do so, because those in charge began to require less and less from the students, and more and more from the part-time faculty. Perhaps this was done pragmatically, as a means of retaining students. Whatever was the reason, I disagreed with the approach. I believe that students should be encouraged to use their brain; they must be encouraged to learn. They should not be mollycoddled. Put succinctly, if the student is hungry, and I give him/her a fish, he/she will eat for a meal. If I teach him/her how to fish, he/she will eat forever!

I encountered day-division students, who had failed a math course, and enrolled in an evening-division math course, because they believed that lesser standards applied in evening-division courses. Of course, as a former day-division instructor, I did not hold any such view. I used the same standards, regardless of which division the students were registered in.

Overall, I have one major disappointment with regard to Seneca. It is the disparity that I observed between its claim of encouraging ethnic diversity, and actual practice — especially as it pertains to the non-promotion of blacks.

During my 5 years as a full-time faculty member, there was a number of highly qualified black faculty at Seneca. Four of them had PhDs, and the rest had Masters' degrees. Yet, not a single black occupied the position of Chair in any department. And when the position for Dean of our department was advertised, one of my black colleagues, Bill Quansah (who has a Ph.D. in mechanical engineering, from a prestigious English university) submitted his application. By noon of the day that he applied, he had received a written rejection of his application. Incidentally, the successful applicant, chosen to fill the Deanship, lasted less than 6 months in the position.

Another black colleague, Norm Williams (who has a Ph.D. in Chemical Engineering) undertook writing the course descriptions and coordinating courses in the evening division technology program. Yet he was never invited to fill any real administrative position, even though vacancies in two such positions occurred during my time there.

In his 1992 mission statement, Steve Quinlan (Seneca's 3rd President) said in part.... *"Diversity is here and it's here to stay. The greatest areas of diversity has been cultural diversity...."*. Then he went on to point out that some 72 languages can be heard throughout the Seneca hallways. He concludes by noting that Seneca's vanguard role is due… *"Thanks to exceptional faculty and staff."* Quinlan said that he was… *"Proud that the College has maintained its ability to attract, retain and motivate those who work for the College, especially the faculty."*

I point out these facts, not because I want to rant about the past. Rather, I do so in the hope that the exclusionary policy that I observed at Seneca, will be changed in the future.

Earlier, I digressed from describing my work as a member of the DQTC, in order to discuss my years at Seneca. Now I will elaborate on my 3-years on the DQTC.

The Ontario Ministry of Health (OMH) provides drugs (listed in its Formulary) to all eligible participants of The Drug Benefits Plan (DBP) , at the Best Available Price (BAP). Generic drugs are usually substantially cheaper than name-brand drugs. Therefore, preference is given to supplying beneficiaries of the BDP with the generic version of the drug, provided that it is shown to be bioequivalent to the name-brand drug.

This is where the DQTC came in. We had to decide,

on the basis of the data submitted, whether or not the generic drug was bioequivalent to the name-brand drug. Bioequivalence of a generic drug is demonstrated when a chemically equivalent drug, in the same dosage form, elicit the same pharmacological response, as the name-brand drug. Invariably, bioequivalence implies therapeutic-equivalence. In such cases, the drugs are said to be interchangeable, whereupon the generic drug would be recommended for listing in the Fomulary.

I will not go into exactly what criteria are used to determine bioequivalence in drugs. All I will say, is that the criteria are stringent. Remember the stakes are very high — not only in terms of the large amount of money involved — but also because of the health implications. So a recommendation (by the DQTC) to list a drug in the Formulary, is not made lightly.

Sometimes the submitting firm became impatient and even aggressive in seeking to have their product listed in the Formulary. This was true of both the name brand and the generic drug manufacturer. And both were not averse to bringing a legal suit against the **OMH** over the **DQTC's** rejection of their submission, if they felt that their submission was not dealt with properly. But while DQTC members were aware of this possibility, we made every effort to not let it influence our decision, one way or another.

There is one particularly memorable DQTC drug submission examination with which I was involved. A generic drug firm retained a consultant to be the spokesperson in support of a drug that they had submitted for listing in the Formulary. The consultant had both a Ph.D. and an M.D degree. In addition, he had authored some 400 publications. I was asked to be one of the examiners of the submission. The first thing I did was to clarify in my mind what I had been asked to decide. It was to decide the merit or otherwise of the submission. It was not to decide on the qualifications of the consultant.

I decided to examine the submission on the following basis. The claims were either —

    a) factual

    b) speculative

         or

    c) self-serving

When I examined the submission, using the above

criteria, I found that there was not a single factual claim in the documents. Instead, there were self-serving statements like 'everyone knows that our product is efficacious....' Well I was not one of those who knew any such thing. I do not recall any of the other statements in support of the submission. But I do recall that the DQTC unanimously rejected the submission.

I also mentioned that the submitting firms (whether name brand or generic) were not above using legal pressure in an attempt to expedite acceptance of their submissions. As an aside, I found that female lawyers were usually far more aggressive than were male lawyers, in pressing for listing of their client's products. Why? I do not know.

Another aspect of my DQTC work involved dealing with so-called Information Letters (IL), circulated by the federal Health Protection Branch (HPB). The HPB sought input from both health professionals and public-advocacy groups, to resolve health problems identified in their ILs. In this way, it was hoped that the problem could be solved, or at least be ameliorated. For example, one of the problems identified (in an IL) was consumer concern over the non-disclosure of non-medical ingredients in drug products.

Unfortunately, the IL was usually replete with governmental verbiage — so much so, as to make them almost unintelligible. So DQTC members were asked for recommendations as to how to make the messages contained in the ILs more easily understood.

Another problem that I had to deal with (as a member of the DQTC), was the excessive and disproportionate cost of different dosages of a given drug. The solution I proposed, was to eliminate all but the least costly dosage of the drug from the Formulary. But this solution is not always appropriate, because in some instances, it is neither convenient nor practical for the user to subdivide the dosage — especially low dosages of highly potent drugs. Nevertheless it was clear that, eliminating the multiplicity of drug dosages in the Formulary would result in a substantial drug-cost saving.

As I said earlier, I found my 3 years on the DQTC to be extremely stimulating. When my appointment was concluded (in 1989), I received a very nice commemorative book on multinational drug issues. The dedication in the book was signed by Elinor Caplan (the Ontario Minister of

Health), Dr, Martin Barkin (the Deputy Minister of Health), Mary Catherine Lindberg (Assistant Deputy Minister), Dr. Jake Thiessen (Chairman-DQTC), and Yale Drazin (Director- Drug Programs Branch).

What about my other professional development? Well, in April 1988, I was elected a Fellow of the Chemical Institute of Canada (FCIC). I regard this as being my official imprimatur as a chemist, by Canada's learned society of chemists.

It is difficult to tell about each important event that took place in my life, in the exact chronological order that it occurred. So I'll go back to August 1987, when Clemmie persuaded me to accompany her on a trip to London, England. I had absolutely no desire to visit London. Back in 1975, when I was enroute home from my consultancy in Milan, London was suggested as a desirable stopover destination. Instead, much to my regret, I chose to stopover in Paris. I didn't really enjoy Paris, and left after three days. So I expected London to be stiff and thoroughly unappealing. What a pleasant surprise awaited me! From the moment we landed at Heathrow airport, and were conveyed to Victoria station (where I got my first real glimpse of London), I was entranced with the city. We had booked accommodations at the Kennedy Hotel, near to Euston Station. It was a moderately priced (but very comfortable hotel), that provided a very adequate breakfast, that was certainly more than a so-called 'continental breakfast'. Clemmie and I each bought a 7-day pass that allowed us to travel extensively on both buses and the subway. We also bought passes to the 'Culture Bus', that took us to 20 sights in London. After we completed the grand 'Culture Bus' tour, we then decided which of the sights we would re-visit at our leisure. As I said earlier, everything about London pleased me. And I was surprised at how good the restaurant food was. I had some of the best rack of ribs I have ever tasted, at a restaurant in Soho. It was so good, that I left an unusually large tip.

We made a side trip to Windsor Castle, and also to Brighton, where my late bother James was stationed, for a time, during World War II. I think that during our 8-day stay, Clemmie and I saw just about every sight that one should see in London. We also had a great view of the changing of the guard directly in front of Buckingham Palace, which was fully explained to us by a staunch

Londoner, who asked us to call him Uncle Bill. I even managed to obtain tickets to a play — 'The Great White Hope' — which we both enjoyed.

A momentous event occurred to Clemmie and me in 1988. That year, in the course of one day, we became instant grandparents! How? Through the process of adoption!

Sharleen and her husband had postponed having children for nearly 10 years, while both of them pursued their professional careers. But for the latter two years, they had tried unsuccessfully to start a family. Then suddenly one day, Sharleen received a call from an adoption agency, telling her that a 3-month baby boy was available for adoption. But the catch was that she had to make up her mind by noon that day! Almost in a panic, Sharleen telephoned both her husband and us, to get our respective take on this unexpected development. We agreed unhesitatingly, and provided her with a written statement to that effect — something required by the adoption agency. Emeka, her husband also gave his consent. So that day, they had a 3-month old son, and we had a 3-month old grandson. I will spare you the details of how both families coped with getting clothing, bedding and all the other activities necessitated by the arrival of a new baby in the home. But simply put, things were hectic ! I will have more to say about changes within our family structure later on. But now I want to return to telling about something else significant that took place in 1988.

That year, I became involved as a mathematics instructor, with the Saturday morning tutorial program at Vaughan Road Collegiate Institute. The program was sponsored by the York Board of Education, and was spearheaded by The Canadian Alliance of Black Educators (CABE). I had seen an announcement about this activity, in SHARE (a local Black-owned newspaper), and decided to offer my services to the program. So I approached the program director John Vieira, to let him know of my willingness to tutor in the program. John accepted my offer enthusiastically, and assigned me to tutor upper-level students (grades 11 to OAC) in mathematics. The program was geared towards black students, and indeed most of the students and tutors were black. But it would be incorrect to say that all the students were black. We had several white students, and also some Chinese students, from time to time. And the students came from as far away as Mississauga and Richmond Hill, even though the York Board of Education sponsored the program.

As I pointed out, in discussing my teaching days at Seneca, I do not believe in spoon-feeding students. I believe that while I had a stake in teaching, they had a stake in learning. So when I tutored at Vaughan Road, I insisted that the student stand with me, at the blackboard, while we went over the solution to their problem. I did this for two reasons. First, because I believe that students function better on their feet — and especially when they are required to participate in finding the solution. Second, because by doing the problem on the blackboard, the other students could also share in learning how to solve the problem. Throughout my tutoring, I always emphasized that I was not interested in the answer. I was interested in teaching students how to approach solving of problems. In so-called 'word problems', my maxim was … ' *If a picture is worth a thousand words, then a thousand words are worth a picture.*' So I tried to have the students make a sketch of the problem, whenever possible. And most important of all, to find out exactly what is the problem, before attempting to solve it. In other words— **define the problem**.

Saturday Morning Tutorial (Vaughan Road Collegiate): (1990)

I cannot tell you how many students I tutored during the 8 years that I participated in the Saturday morning program. All told, they numbered in the hundreds. But of all these, there are only four students that I remember vividly. Perhaps coincidentally they were two brother and sister pairs. Unfortunately, I cannot recall the name of the first brother and sister pair who made such an impression on me. But I do recall that the brother was enrolled at Trent University (in Peterborough) and the sister attended the University of Toronto, after finishing the Vaughan Road tutorial Program. Why did they impress me? Well it was because both of these students were attending school under less than ideal circumstances. Whenever I called their home, to convey some information pertaining to a problem we had encountered (but did not resolve) during the tutorial session, invariably our conversation was interrupted by wailing and other distractions, from their younger siblings. Yet these two elder family members pressed on determinedly with their studies. I was particularly impressed with the sister. Before she enrolled at the U. of T., I told her about something that they do not teach at any university. I call it *'The Care and Management of University Professors'*. It is something that every university student should be aware of.

I won't say exactly what I told her in this context, but she heeded my advice fully. When I met her some time after she had started at the U. of T., she rushed up to me, thanking me for the advice I had given her regarding university professors. She assured me that it was working well.

I do recall the name of the other brother and sister siblings who impressed me. They are Stanley and Belinda Munro. I tutored both of them for several years, in the Saturday morning program. But I had much more to do with Stanley, than with Belinda.

I had the pleasure of attending Stanley's U. of T. convocation in June of 2000. Now he is enrolled in a Masters of Education program at Johns Hopkins University, in Baltimore. He keeps in touch with me regularly by telephone and e-mail. Ultimately, he plans to pursue a doctorate in Education.

Belinda also graduated from the U. of T. in the Fall of 2000. She is now pursuing a singing career in Atlanta, Georgia.

These four students represent (at least to me) limited successes, for the substantial effort expended by all the tutors in the program. What disappointed me, was the lack of commitment on the part of too many of the students. Most wanted just a 'quick fix' to get them through the next test, instead of having the desire for **long-term learning**. During my years in the program, I tried vainly to instill this desire in the students. But except for the students that I mentioned earlier, mostly I failed to do so.

Several times, at the conclusion of the tutorial year, I was asked to give the closing remarks. On such occasions, I would try to leave various witticisms with the students. Some of the things I said were ——

- ➤ **The only place success comes before work, is in the dictionary.**
- ➤ **If you think that education is expensive, try ignorance.**
- ➤ **It is better to light one candle, than to curse the darkness.**
- ➤ **People who replace 'wish bone' with 'back bone' pave their road to success.**
- ➤ **Worry is the price we pay, for the problems we seldom have.**

After some 8 years in the program, I decided to quit. I had had enough of being disappointed at not being able to motivate more students. However, In retrospect, I should not have been surprised that I had not been able to *'turn the students on'* to the study of mathematics, as it were. After all, at most I had them collectively for less than

3 hours each week, and individually for no more than half an hour. By the time that they came for tutoring, they had been thoroughly *'turned off'* from mathematics, thanks to the ponderous curriculum and abstruse mathematics texts to which they had been subjected.

I had seen how *'turned off'* from mathematics the students were, while I was a full time faculty member at Seneca. And this aversion to mathematics persists to this day. You may ask why? I believe that the answer is that the relevance of mathematics to daily life is not taught in our schools. Instead, mathematics is simply imposed as a subject that has to be taken for a senior school credit. Calculus is a universal part of the mathematics curriculum. But I doubt if 2% of the students, who take it, could explain accurately what Calculus is. Moreover, few if any of them will ever use it any time in the future.

In 1992, I tried to urge for corrective measures, when I participated (as a member of the Interpretation Panel), in a review of the Grade 10 - General Level curriculum. At the end of four intensive 3 to 4 hour sessions, the panel made recommendations to the board. As I recall it, our recommendations emerged as part of a feckless report, full of the usual pedagogical jargon. Nothing was about to change. And you wonder why the students continue to be *'turned off'* about mathematics? Well enough about that. Let's get on with other matters.

1990 was another banner year in our family's life. That year, Sharleen gave birth to our granddaughter, Adora. So we were now grandparents for the second time. Our grandson Dike (or Adam as he prefers to be called) was now 2- years old. In addition, Sharleen also received her MSW degree from York University. Two momentous events in the same year. Her thesis advisor wanted Sharleen to continue for the Ph.D. degree, but I advised her against doing so. I pointed out to her that she had devoted many years to school. Now she had a family. It was time to devote more time to them.

I will now fast forward two years, to 1992 — a year that was memorable for two reasons. First, that year, a disaffected Concordia University professor murdered four of his colleagues, allegedly because he had been denied tenure. Second, 1992 marked the 45th anniversary of my graduation from Sir George Williams — one of the two institutions that amalgamated (in 1974) to form Concordia

University.

I was so mortified by the repugnance of a professor murdering his colleagues — that I wanted to disassociate myself from anything having to do with Concordia. Yet, as a lifelong 'Georgian', I wanted to associate myself with my 'alma mater' (which still exists in my mind, regardless of the amalgamation) in her time of trauma. So I decided that I would attend the September 1992 Homecoming exercises at Concordia.

I drove down to Montreal alone, and stayed 4 days with my brother Michael, and his wife Lilleth. Once there, I talked Michael into attending the Homecoming, since it marked the 30th anniversary of his graduation from Sir George. Despite the tragic aura that permeated the Rector's dinner (the crowning Homecoming event), overall it was well worth attending. At the dinner, I was interviewed for about 30 minutes (by some television personnel) about my days at Sir George. A greatly abridged version of my remarks was presented in a Concordia publicity video called **'Real Education For The Real World'**.

The day after the Concordia Rector's dinner, Michael and Lilleth hosted an impromptu get together at their place.

It was the first time in years that all six members of my family were in the same room. Fortunately, pictures were taken of the occasion, for it marked the last time that we were ever together.

With My Siblings: (1992)

On December 22, 1999, my elder brother James passed away suddenly and unexpectedly. He had just observed his 79th birthday, on November 22. And roughly 18 months later, my eldest sister Helen (who had moved to New York City, more than 40 years ago) passed away there, on June 8, 2001. So there are now four surviving members of my family.

Now to continue the story.

My mandatory retirement from Seneca (in 1991) made it necessary for me to seek outlets for either consulting opportunities, or other income-producing activity. One option was to attempt to do further teaching. So, I approached The Dean of Continuing Education, (Faculty of Engineering) at the University of Toronto, with a proposal to teach a course entitled '**Process Cost Estimation**', that I had developed. I had had plenty of experience in preparing project cost-estimates, during my days at Canada Packers. Therefore I felt confident that I could provide the Engineering students (that I would be teaching), with valuable insights about this topic.

After reviewing my proposal, the University decided to offer the course in the 92/93 session.

Unfortunately, due to unfavourable economic conditions at the time, there was insufficient registration for the proposed course; hence the course did not run.

An epochal event occurred in 1994. On December 10th, my father-in-law Mr. Tuitt (or Dad Tuitt as I called him), reached his 100th birthday. His wife Edna hosted a gala catered party (at St. Paul's L'Amoreaux Centre), where they had lived since 1978. Over 125 relatives and friends, some of whom had come from as far away as California, attended the birthday party. My brother-in-law Allan (Dr. Allan MacKenzie, who kindly wrote a foreword to this memoir) was the emcee. Dad Tuitt's birthday was acknowledged with greetings from:- Her Majesty Queen Elizabeth, the Governor General (Hon. Ray Hnatyshyn), the Prime Minister (Rt. Honourable Jean Chrétien), the Lt.-Governor of Ontario (His Honour Mr. Jackman), the Premier of Ontario (Hon. Bob Rae), the member of parliament for Scarborough-Agincourt (Mr.Karygiannis), the MPP (Mr. Gerry Phillips), and the City Councillor (Mr. Ron Watson).

My role at the party was to tell some anecdotes about Dad Tuitt, to illustrate how, in my view, *'he had beaten the odds'.* Here are two of my favourite of his anecdotes. The first had to do with World War I. As he related it to me, it was the first day that he had come under artillery fire from the Germans. A Major kept going up and down the Canadian lines, telling the troops that they had nothing to be afraid about. However, this did not reassure Dad Tuitt. He told me he was so scared, that if a two-

penny nail had been shoved up his anus, ***the nail's head
would have been bitten off!*** Shortly after that, Dad Tuitt
was reassigned to the Quartermaster's stores (because of
trench foot); therefore, he did not come under artillery fire
for the balance of the war. So, as a result, he beat the odds,
by surviving the war.

The other anecdote has to do with the longevity of
his retirement. When Dad Tuitt retired from the CPR, after
working there for 40 years as a sleeping car porter, he was
offered a part-time job by one of the supervisors there. The
person who offered the job told him that … ***'It is better to
wear out, than to rust out.'*** Dad Tuitt told me that he
thanked the man for having made the offer. But he
confided to me, that he had absolutely no intention of ever
working again. And he never did. Again, he beat the odds
— this time by being retired for 35 years, in good health,
for all but roughly the last two months of his life. He
passed away on January 11, 1996, one month and one day
after his 101st birthday.

Late in June 1995, Sharleen and Emeka invited us to
accompany them (and our two grandchildren), on a trip to
Atlantic Canada. We were not sure why they had asked us

to go on the trip with them. Usually, younger couples don't like having *'old fogies'* along — especially in-laws, in Emeka's case. Was it so as to have built-in babysitters? Or was it to have co-drivers on the trip, since both Clemmie and I could drive a car? Whatever the reason (and encouraged by Sharleen's assurances that they really wanted us along), we agreed to go on the trip. However, we did so primarily because we had neglected Atlantic Canada during our travels. Clemmie had never been there, and I had not been there since my one trip to Halifax, in 1945. Yet we had travelled west in Canada as far as Victoria, BC. So it was 'yes' for the proposed trip.

Sharleen looked after reservations for the trip, and I planned the itinerary. What a great trip we had. We left Toronto in Sharleen and Emeka's 1990 Aerostar van, on Monday, July 17, bound for Rivière du Loup, Quebec. When we arrived at our motel there, nearly 11 hours later, our grandson Adam asked us... *'Did we come all this* way, just to stay in a hotel?' That was the first of many queries that he and our granddaughter Adora would make, during the trip. The next day, we drove to Fredericton, NB. There, we visited several tourist sights, including the

University of New Brunswick (where I had planned to continue my Ph.D. studies in 1956), and also the legislative buildings. After Fredericton, we drove to Moncton, NB where we experienced the optical illusion of the so-called '***Magnetic Hill***'. That is where your car appears to back uphill when it is placed in neutral gear! We were also able to view **The Tidal Bore of The Petitcodiac** while we were in Moncton. It is claimed to be one of the world's great natural wonders.

From Moncton, we drove to Cape Tormentine, where we boarded the ferry for Prince Edward Island. We spent 3 days at the housekeeping unit of the Rodd Royalty Inn, in Charlottetown. This gave us an opportunity to visit **Cavendish** (the home of **Anne of Green Gables** author, Lucy Maud Montgomery), and also see the **Confederation Players 1995 Festival** of **The Fathers** (**of Confederation**). Since we were in PEI, we took the opportunity to indulge our appetite for seafood, especially lobster. But our grandson Adam was drawn to oysters, mussels and shrimp. This gave me an opportunity to remind him that, since he had a caviar appetite, he must take steps (while in school) to assure that he will earn a caviar salary, once he starts working. I never lose the opportunity to remind both of my grandchildren of the importance of getting a good education.

Then we drove to the Woods Island ferry, where island fiddlers and step-dancers entertained us. After watching the step-dancers for a while, Adora, our granddaughter became moderately proficient at this form of dancing.

We took the Woods Island ferry from PEI to Halifax, NS. The city had changed greatly, and was much improved, from when I was last there in 1945. We visited the Citadel, the Botanical Gardens, Peggie's Cove, Dalhousie University and The Black Cultural Centre, in Dartmouth. After 3 days in Halifax, we drove west across Nova Scotia, to Digby, where we boarded the Bay of Fundy ferry for Saint John, NB.

The only thing that I remembered about Saint John, was that in my youth, it was where boxed circular biscuits (roughly 4 inches in diameter, and somewhat like a soda cracker) were sold. These biscuits were delicious, and were not available anywhere else in Canada, as far as I knew. I did not see any during my brief stay in Saint John. But we did see the Reversing Falls —— a sight well worth seeing.

From Saint John, we drove northwest through New Brunswick, into the province of Quebec. We stopped at St. Jean- Port Joli, a town roughly 75 miles east of Quebec City. We had planned to visit Quebec City briefly, the next day, enroute to Montreal, where we were to stopover for a few days. However, Clemmie decided that she would call her parents, perhaps because of an intuition that something might be wrong. When she called, Dad Tuitt told her that her mother was in the North York General Hospital, with a liver disorder. So our plans changed immediately. We decided to drive directly from where we were to Toronto —— a distance of some 550 miles —— by-passing Montreal, and the barbecue that Clemmie's nephew Calvin, had planned for us. On arriving in Toronto, we went directly to the hospital, where Ma Tuitt had been taken the day before. Fortunately, her liver problem responded to treatment, and she was released from the hospital after 3 or 4 days. We had had a great trip to Atlantic Canada, despite the unexpected interruption due to Ma Tuitt's illness. Perhaps we will have an opportunity to visit other places in that part of Canada, sometime in the future.

The trip to Atlantic Canada awakened in me the desire to re-visit other old, once familiar places. So in April 1996, I paid a return visit to l'Université de Montréal, after an absence of 34 years. The occasion was an Organic Chemistry Symposium, organized by Graduate Students of the department of Chemistry. It was a superb symposium — fully the equal of any that I had attended over the years, under the auspices of the American Chemical Society. Some 15 world-class chemists presented papers, either in French or in English. Surprisingly, even though I was no longer conversing regularly in French, I had no difficulty following those papers that were presented in French.

A delightful touch at the symposium, was the mid-morning and mid-afternoon break, during which the attendees could mingle, and even discuss briefly, some topic that had caught their interest. But the crowning event was the ***vin d'honneur***, at the conclusion of the symposium.

A ***vin d'honneur*** is something peculiar to French Canadian academic institutions such as Laval and l'Université de Montréal — something I never experienced during my 3 years at McGill. In my view, it adds a touch of class to, and enhances the conviviality of events such as this.

I enjoyed my 1996 visit to l'Université de Montréal so much, that I eagerly registered for the next symposium held there in 1999. It was just as good as the earlier symposium. And as an added bonus, I had an opportunity to re-connect with some of my 1962 classmates, who were now full-professors, nearing retirement.

In 1997, our daughter Sharleen received her Certification as a Social Worker.

That year was also the 50th year of my B.Sc. graduation from 'Sir George'. I had not planned to attend the Homecoming exercises. But I changed my mind because of two occurrences. First, I was asked to participate in writing a Retrospective (about our days at 'Sir George'), on the 60th anniversary of the First Graduating Class of Sir George Williams College — one of the founding institutions of Concordia University. It was then that I realized that my class (1947) was the 10th graduating class at 'Sir George'. So Clemmie and I decided to attend the Rector's 1997 Commemorative Reunion Dinner. The dinner was held at the St. James Club, on Peel Street, in

Montreal. Only five of my classmates showed up. I was surprised at how old some of them looked. Still, I was glad that I attended. Clemmie met one of her former teachers (from her Business School Days at 'Sir George') — Norman Manson and his wife. He was one of the so-called Guinea Pigs, who comprised the First Graduating Class at 'Sir George'. Dr. Rita Shane (a retired M.D. who was the only female in the First Graduating Class) also attended. They provided many interesting reminiscences from their halcyon days at 'Sir George'. How unlike Concordia, with its penchant for student unrest and violence.

I doubt that I will attend any more Homecomings. The number of surviving class members will undoubtedly decrease, thereby lessening the likelihood that attending such an event will prove to be personally satisfying.

Next, I will turn to a significant event in my professional life that took place in 1999. That year, I decided to dissolve my consulting firm, **INNOCHEM CONSULTANTS LIMITED**. I did so because of a novel way in which potential pharmaceutical products were being screened, starting roughly in 1996. That innovation was something called **Combinatorial Chemistry** — a field that I was not equipped to offer consulting advice in.

I will not go into details as to exactly what this new type of chemistry is. But, in general terms, it affords a rapid, highly-efficient means of screening large numbers of chemical structures, for promising leads to pharmaceutical products. Prior to this development, it was usual that 10,000 compounds would have to be synthesized, before one promising lead compound would be uncovered. The cost of such an approach is astronomical — well in excess of $100-million for each new pharmaceutical product developed. Now, the expectation is that new pharmaceuticals will be discovered much quicker (and less expensively), through the use of Combinatorial Chemistry. So, I was now finally fully retired. It was time to get back to doing a bit of travelling.

A reason for, and an opportunity to travel, came in July 2001— the 50th anniversary of our wedding. Clemmie and I decided to celebrate the occasion by taking a trip to Greece and Turkey. So, we contacted a travel agent, who had been recommended to us by a friend. The trip that she organized for us was called 'Glorious Greece'.

We nearly did not go on the trip. Unknown to us,

Sharleen was planning a large 50th anniversary party for us. She had contacted several hotels, in search of a suitable place for the event. However, (and fortunately for us), our granddaughter let us in on Sharleen's plans accidentally. We had a difficult time persuading Sharleen that, the last thing we wanted, was an anniversary party! But eventually we prevailed. So we were able to recharge our batteries so to speak, by travelling.

The trip consisted of a 4-day, 3-night land tour of Greece, followed by a 7-day cruise to Turkey and 5- Greek islands. It would end with a 3-day stay in Athens.

We observed our 50th anniversary on Saturday July 14th, aboard our cruise ship (the Stella Solaris), which had anchored in Istanbul's harbour.

At dinner that evening, Clemmie and I were serenaded by some of the ship's musicians. Then we were presented with a lovely cake, to mark our wedding anniversary. All in all, it was a very enjoyable anniversary observance.

The only way that I can adequately describe the trip, is to say that it was unforgettable! The places that we visited, and the things we saw (both in Greece and in

Turkey), made this the trip of our lifetime.

Our 50th Anniversary (Istanbul, Turkey): (2001)

At 10:30am, on Monday July 21, we left Athens on a flight to Toronto. We landed in Toronto at 2:00pm, and were processed rapidly through Customs and Immigration. So rapidly indeed, that including the time to recover our luggage, procure an airport limousine and be driven home, we were in our suite exactly 1 hour after landing at Pearson Airport. A wonderful end to a wonderful trip.

CHAPTER EIGHT

EPILOGUE —THE STORY BEHIND THE STORY!

Whenever someone undertakes to write an autobiography, several questions and considerations arise. One question is, why write an autobiography in the first place? Is it motivated at all by egotism? And if you do decide to write about yourself, what do you include, and what do you leave out?

Well, in an attempt to answer these several questions, I will paraphrase Paul Harvey (the noted U.S. radio newscaster and commentator) by saying … *'Here is The Rest of The Story!'*

I had resisted repeated entreaties by my friend (Mr. Justice Romain Pitt, of The Ontario Superior Court of Justice), to write my autobiography. Each time that he brought the subject up, I would say to him … "Romain, who cares about my life story?" His repeated reply was … "Tom, you have a story worth telling!"

Finally, I relented, and decided to write my autobiography. However, once that decision was made, I had several other contingent decisions to make as well.

The first decision was that I was going to be scrupulously honest in whatever I wrote.

Second, it would be my story — not the story of my birth family. I wanted to present the highs and lows of my life, from my perspective. Particularly, I wanted to tell how I, the fourth of my widowed mother's six children dealt with the many challenges in my life. How I managed to get through High School (by age 16), and through to a 4-year college degree (by age 20), without having any money. And I wanted to relate my contrasting graduate school experience at McGill and at l'Université de Montréal. Then I undertook to tell about my life as a Research Chemist and later, as a Pharmaceutical Chemistry Consultant.

I believe that I have met these objectives in the preceding pages of this memoir. Still there were some things that were omitted, in order to tell my story more coherently. Now however, I am going to exercise a writer's prerogative, by telling about someone who became very important in my life — here, virtually at the end of my autobiography. That person's name was Dotty Burgess. She was a girlhood friend of my mother. Both she and Mother came from the West Indian Island of Montserrat. She lived in New York's Harlem — at 102 West 142nd Street.

Dotty Burgess (or Aunt Dot as she became to my siblings and me) and Mother had lost touch with each other, since 1917, when Mother emigrated from Montserrat to Montreal (Canada). But sometime around 1940, they re-established contact with each other. Initially, my elder sisters (Helen and Margaret) went to visit Aunt Dot in New York. Eventually, all the other members of my family (except me) made visits to her home. She gave each of them a complete set of keys to her apartment. There was no need to alert her that you were coming for a visit. Just show up, and you were made welcome! As I said earlier, I was the only member of my family who had never been to

Aunt Dot's home. In fact, I had never even met her.

Either in October or November 1945, Aunt Dot paid us a visit to Montreal. When she met me, she asked me why I had never been to New York. I told her that it was because I had to work on holidays (such as Christmas, Easter and especially during the summer vacation from school), in order to earn some money for my schooling. She then asked me … "If I send you a train ticket to New York, would you come and visit me at Christmas?" I assured her that I would do so, even though I did not believe that she would actually send me a train ticket. Well surprise! surprise! On December 15th, I received a round trip ticket to New York, valid on the Delaware and Hudson train that ran out of Montreal daily. I left for New York on December 17th, for an 18-day visit to New York.

Aunt Dot spoiled me rotten during my stay. She saw to my every need. Nearly every day, she gave me $10.00 — a princely amount in those days of a 5-cents subway ride, and when $1.00 bought a lavish meal at the Horn and Hardart Automat.

I visited every worthwhile sight in each of the five boroughs that comprise New York City. One day I would visit educational institutions. Another day it would be museums. Then I would go to see various entertainment centres such as Carnegie Hall, and the Metropolitan Opera House. Later, I went to Radio City Music Hall to see Bing Crosby, Ingrid Bergman and Barry Fitzgerald in The Bells of St. Mary, then watched enthralled, as The Rockettes performed their Christmas show.

This is how I spent the first of many visits that I made to Aunt Dot's home. With each visit, increasingly, she showered me with unfettered love. Soon, it seemed (at least to me) that I was probably her favourite among my siblings. She was present for two especially significant events in my life — my B.Sc. graduation, and my wedding. And she enthusiastically acknowledged each success that came my way. But most importantly, she accepted me as I was — warts, molds and all! I could do no wrong in her eyes. This unencumbered acceptance was something that I (a sensitive and introspective person) needed — and still cherish to this day.

Aunt Dot passed away in 1978. To me, she will always be someone who was special in my life. One of the last photos I have of her is shown on the next page.

Aunt Dot: (1949)

Today, as I look back on the long, arduous path that I took to become the person that I am today, I marvel at my tenacity in sticking to my goals. The one characteristic that accurately describes me, is summarized in the U. S. Marine's motto *'Semper Fidelis'* ... *'Always Faithful'* — in my case, to my goals in life. I hope that I have been able to convey this in the preceding pages of this autobiography.

In concluding this memoir, I want to say a special thanks to two people — my late Mother, and my wife.

Thanks Mother for instilling unquenchable ambition

in me during my formative years, then allowing me to follow my academic pursuits for the 15 years that it took for me to obtain my B.Sc. degree. My debt of gratitude to you is undiminished, even after the more than 35 years since you passed away.

And finally, I want to thank my wife Clemmie, for giving me so much more of herself, than I deserved at times, during more than 50 years of marriage. She is the person who kept me on an even keel — who kept my natural volatility in check. She has helped me to buy into the truism that … *'Even God cannot change the past'*. Through her, I came to realize that you have a choice. You can use the hurts in life to grow bitter, or you can use them to get better. And while it is important to learn from the past, there is a real danger in focusing too much on the past. Remember another truism … *'You can never catch up with the past, even if you try running backwards!'* So while I try to learn from the past, my constant focus is on the future — thanks to Clemmie's constant admonitions.

How do I sum up the 70 years I have described, in what has been for me, a very eventful life? I will say that they have been filled with changing opinions, but of unchanging hope in the essential decency of Man. So, I will continue to be an optimist, and encourage you, the reader to do as Browning proposed, namely —

'Grow old along with me!

The best is yet to be'

APPENDIX A

Addendum to:

Musings of a Native Son
- An Autobiography.

In my autobiography, I point out that my acceptance of 'black' in describing my ethnicity came during a visit to Texas Southern University in 1971. But on further reflection, I recall an incident that probably provided the catalyst for the change in my psyche, whereby I embraced the term 'black' as a descriptor, when thinking or speaking about my people. That incident occurred in 1962, shortly after I joined Ayerst Research Laboratories.

I received a telephone call. The caller asked to speak to Dr. Massiah. I replied ... " Speaking!". He told me that he was calling to sell me a life-insurance policy. When he identified the insurance company that he was representing,

I asked him if the company had any restrictive clauses in the policies they were offering. I knew that this company did have policies that blacks were excluded from buying. The caller replied to my query by saying … "Oh that does not apply to you!". I asked him … "Why?". He said … "You don't sound like a coloured man to me!". I continued by asking him … "And what does a coloured man sound like?". Mortified, the caller realized (all too late), that he had 'put his foot in his mouth' so to speak. I ended his discomfiture by suggesting an appropriate repository for the life insurance policy that he had called me about.

I should point out that, subsequently, I did obtain a preferred life policy from the same insurance company that had excluded blacks from such policies.

However, the policy was granted only after a Jewish insurance broker Bernie Rubenstein threatened to publicize the company's exclusionary practice towards blacks.

I was neither surprised nor especially angered by the ignorance and insensitivity displayed by the caller. After all, back then, we were simply 'coloured people', with all the negative connotations associated with the term. That is why I found it necessary (in my autobiography) to explain what informed blacks understand and wish to have understood when we use black today, in describing ourselves.

APPENDIX B

Connections
by
Thomas F. Massiah, B.Sc. ('47)

Several years ago, I read an intriguing story about some holocaust survivors. The details are somewhat vague in my mind, but I do recall the essence of their story. It involved some Polish Jews, who were inmates (during World War II) in one of the most infamous Nazi death camps. Daily, there were deaths among the inmates, caused by disease, starvation and the inhumane work conditions. Yet, some 20 or so of the inmates survived the incarceration. How? Well, despite the forbidding setting, this group met secretly (over the protracted imprisonment) to discuss music. This as it turned out was their survival connection. Their almost unbelievable survival story, prompted me to share a remotely similar personal story with you.

In 1944, during my undergraduate years at Sir George, I (along with other male students) was required to join the reserve army. Our unit was an artillery regiment, headquartered in the Craig Street armoury, near to the Montreal City Hall. That summer, we were sent to Picton, Ontario for two weeks of live artillery training.

I was assigned to the 5th battery, while others of my fellow students were sent to the 12th battery. It seemed that there were more non students in the 12th battery (than true of the 5th battery), and they seemed to be more roughly hewn. In any event, at night (when we were at liberty, so to speak), drinking and gambling was a constant occurrence within the 12th battery tent lines. Almost mysteriously, several members of the 12th battery (who were disinclined to what was going on there), began to meet in tents of the 5th battery to talk. I do not know who initiated the get-together, nor do I recall precisely what we talked about. What I do recall however, is that each conversation was stimulating — so much so, that we always looked forward to our next session.

Years later, I thought back to those conversations and wondered what had happened to the participants. I discovered a remarkable fact. Each of us had gone on to obtain a doctorate, albeit in different disciplines. Obviously, we had established some sort of enduring career-inducing connection, as a result of our army-camp discussions. And although we were never in a life-threatening situation (unlike the holocaust survivors mentioned earlier), in a sense, our discussions had a life-sustaining effect.

Who are the other four members of our discussion group? They are Ralph Pelley (B.Sc. '45), Russell Blackmore (B. Sc. '46), Fernand Perron (B.Sc. '46) and the late Doug McFarlane (B.Sc. '46).

APPENDIX C

DOES TRAINING IN THE SCIENCES LEAD TO AGNOSTICISM?

by

Thomas F. Massiah, B.Sc., M.Sc., Ph.D.

[Published in Postgrad (June 1963) Sir George Williams University]

For some time now, I have pondered this question, and while I am still no closer to a definitive answer concerning it, I am prepared to do what we are taught to do in science, namely — consider the facts. First, let me relate however, why I should be pondering such a question in the first place.

Whenever I have expressed honest doubt about or questioned anything written in the Bible, invariably I have been admonished with a blanket condemnation... that '...you 'scientists' always think you know all the answers!', and... '...were it not for you 'scientists', the world would not be in the mess that it is in!'.

Although I cannot presume to the lofty title of being a 'scientist', I am by training and inclination, a student of the sciences — and with no other qualification other than the fact of my inclination towards the sciences, I am going to present my views on behalf of the scientists concerning the foregoing admonitions, and the question posed initially.

Let me say right away, that no scientist worthy of the name believes that he (or she) knows all the answers. In fact, it is precisely for the opposite reason — namely,— that he does not know most of the answers, that he engages in the business of being a scientist. As a scientist, he must rigorously apply the scientific method to anything that comes within his experience. He must rigorously examine all things in the light of his awareness of these things without bias — accepting what is consistent with known facts, and rejecting what is inconsistent. This does not mean however, that science is an inflexible, rigid discipline. Quite the opposite is true. While the methods of science are rigid and inflexible, scientific thought, ideas, concepts and hypotheses are being modified constantly — but the modification is always done in the light of new facts.

I have often heard it said '…well you used to believe such and such, how come you no longer believe this?' This is as it should be. In order to be truly scientific, one must be constantly putting one's house in order, as it were. To do so requires a constant re-examining of the views which one has held on a particular point. Truth is the essence of science, and a truth must be true everywhere, or it is not true anywhere. It is the constant searching after truth which tends to stigmatize scientists, in the eyes of so many people, as being necessarily atheists at the worst, or agnostics at the very least. Yet it is the searching out of truth, that is the scientist's eternal task.

What about the other matter, namely that — '…were it not for you 'scientists', the world wouldn't be in the mess that it is in' ?. This accusation is so widespread, that I have noticed that, at least two of my colleagues have seemingly embraced this idea, and have sought solace for their conscience by turning increasingly towards the Humanities. Now lest the Humanists misinterpret the intention of my remark, let me hasten to state that I have no quarrel with the Humanities. I believe that it is good for Man to have an introspective side. I think that it is good for Man to ponder such abstractions as the Good, the True and the Beautiful. I think that it is good for Man to ponder whence and whither. But contemplative, introspective activity alone, or mouthing of idealistic platitudes, will not build bridges, harness hydroelectric power, conquer space, or produce so many other advances in technology and public health, as to defy enumeration. No, it is not science that has the world in a mess! It is the misuse of science by non-scientists, which has laid bare the threat that Man may destroy himself within our lifetime. The development, (by scientists), of the capacity by Man to release thermonuclear energy, was not, in my view, intended by the scientists who worked on 'the bomb', for use against Man. Rather, it is my conviction that by developing such a horrendous article as atomic bomb, they hoped that it would be possible to shock Man into accepting the ultimatum — 'Peace in the world, or the world in pieces!'

I tire of people who try to define the boundaries for scientific exploration. There is a great hue and cry in evidence today,— that here we are probing outer space, when we have so many problems that are begging for a solution here on earth. Why go to the Moon, when we haven't conquered cancer or heart disease? Why should we spend billions on developing more heinous weapons of destruction, when two-thirds of the world's population goes to bed hungry every night?

I cannot answer these questions, which are socio-euthenic, and could be better answered by a social scientist.

I can attempt however, to answer the criticism, as to the extent to which Man should probe the unknown. My answer is simply this. I believe that the extent of Man's probing should be defined only by the limits of his imagination. Suppose that Columbus had continued to believe that the earth was flat? Or suppose that Paul Erlich, Louis Pasteur, Joseph Lister, Newton, Galileo, Einstein, Fermi, or any of the great scientists had ceased to probe? Suppose that each, in his time, had adopted the view that, what was then known, represented all that was to be known? The answer to this query is obvious. If we knew enough in the 17th century to have ceased our probing there, we would have to accept 17th century Public Health standards today, for example. Need I protract my point further?

Now let us turn to the fundamental question — **Does Training in Science Lead to Agnosticism?** As I stated at the outset, I cannot give a definitive answer. What I can say, is that as a disciple of science, it is my contention that anything that is presented for widespread acceptance, must be supported by the weight of evidence. Otherwise, it is either to be rejected outright, or at least held in abeyance. This, I think represents the position of many of us who are engaged in the field of science. We don't know, and not knowing, we cannot either accept or reject. In this sense, therefore, we are agnostic. I must however temper the term somewhat, in that it seems to be too severe a term to truly describe our position. It is not as though we are playing it safe, by adopting a wait-and-see attitude. Rather it is that we have not been able to fully evaluate the evidence presented. On the one hand, one cannot investigate any field of science and not be impressed with, indeed amazed by, the orderliness of events. Such order could hardly been by chance.

Yet it is this very order which makes it difficult, if not altogether impossible, for us to accept an anthropomorphic view of God. Can any of us say truly that he can imagine a unique being, who can control, at one and the same time, all of the myriad complex functions which occur simultaneously throughout the universe, in a given instant? Theologians will say that it is a matter of faith. They will tell you that it is written — that there are ecclesiastical things which are beyond man's capacity to ponder. The scientist adopts the position that the alleged celestial mediation of events has not been proved, and in the absence of proof, such claims must be held in abeyance. Is this agnosticism? Perhaps it is, but personally, I do not think it is quite that.

You see, as I stated earlier, the scientific method permits one to accept something as a working hypothesis, subject of course to its validity being demonstrated ultimately, by some tangible proof, in order for it to be retained within the framework of what is acceptable as a scientific truth. Thus it is not inconsistent for a scientist to accept the concept of God, as a working hypothesis. The extent to which he requires proof of the validity of his hypothesis and its persistence, will be largely an individual matter. What is invariant among scientists however, is that,— what is accepted as being true, must be true universally, or it is not true anywhere. This test is, therefore, a sufficient test to safeguard against inconsistency in the application of the scientific method, even to things allegedly celestial. Science must not make exceptions to the rigorous application of this precept, for if it makes an exception in one instance, then why not more than one, or whenever one has a mind to?

There are arguments for, and counter-arguments to the views which I have expressed, and I have used a large number of words to say this. I feel that it is inescapable, that as one probes more deeply into the realm of science, one tends to be less positive about anything. One learns to adopt the position which is supported by the greatest weight of evidence, realizing full well that, new evidence might undermine, if not totally destroy, a position that was held formerly.

OTHER ARTICLES

By

T. F. Massiah

1. Massiah, T.F., 'To PhD Or Not To PhD', Faculty Newsletter, p.12 –16 (December 1963).
2. Massiah, T.F., 'Quality Teaching Comes From The Heart', Letter to The Editor, Toronto Star (August 1972).
3. Massiah, T.F., 'Think Positively', Letter to The Editor, C & EN, p.18 (August 21, 1972).
4. Massiah, T.F., 'Mortgage-Related Calculations', Chemical Engineering, p. 109-112 (October 3, 1983).
5. Massiah, T.F., 'How To Store And Retrieve Technical Articles', Chemical Engineering, p.71-74 (August 19, 1985).
6. Massiah, T.F., 'Are We Preparing Our Students

Adequately For The Technological Challenges Of The 1990s?', A Talk Presented At Queen's University, CHEM ED 89 (August 14, 1989).

7. Massiah, T.F., 'Consultants: An Unnecessary Expense or A Cost-Effective Benefit?, PSG News 2(2) (Spring 1990).

8. Massiah, T.F., 'Winning At Research And Development', Chemical Engineering, p.127-134 (July 1992).

9. Massiah, T.F., 'Recycling Human Resources As A Way To Help Small Business', Canadian Chemical News(ACCN), p.12 (February 1995).

10. Massiah, T.F., 'Reminiscences On Outstanding Teachers', in 'On the 60th Anniversary Of the First Graduating Class Of Sir George Williams University: A Retrospective (1997).'

11. Massiah, T.F., 'A Perspective On Science And The Public', Canadian Chemical News (ACCN), p.26 (May 2001).

12. Massiah, T.F., 'Thoughts On Enhancing The Public Image Of Chemistry', Canadian Chemical News (ACCN), p.14 (July/August 2001).

13. Massiah, T.F., 'Caveats On Genetic Research: A Response To 'Que Sera Sera'', Concordia University Magazine, p.4 (December 2001).

14. Massiah, T.F., 'Understanding Acid Rain: Its Consequences and Proposed Remedies', The Crest, p.4 (June 2002).

15. Massiah, T.F., 'Water: Nature's Most Versatile Chemical', The Crest, p.3 (July/August 2002).

16. Massiah, T.F., 'Drugs: Name-Brand Or Generic/', The Crest, p.5 (September 2002).

17. Massiah, T.F., 'Plastics: Definition, Examples And Environmental Consequences', The Crest, p.5 (October 2002).

18. Massiah, T.F., 'Global Warming: Fact Or Fiction?', The Crest, p.5 (November 2002).

19. Massiah, T.F., 'Cholesterol: Its Functions, Its Role In Heart Disease, And Its Control', The Crest, p.7 (February 2003).

20. Massiah, T.F., 'DNA: Its Use In Fighting Crime', The Crest, p.3 (March 2003).

INDEX: